CRYPTO INV

How to Invest in Bitc ..., NFTs, and More

By Ian Balina and the Token Metrics Team

TOKEN
METRICS

ISBN 978-1-7373021-0-0 (Hardcover Edition)
ISBN 978-1-7373021-2-4 (Paperback Edition)
ISBN 978-1-7373021-1-7 (Ebook Edition)

DISCLAIMER

Token Metrics Media LLC is a regular publication of information, analysis, and commentary focused primarily on blockchain technology and business, cryptocurrency, blockchain-based tokens, market trends, and trading strategies.

Token Metrics Media LLC does not provide individually tailored investment advice and does not take a subscriber's or anyone's circumstances into consideration when discussing investments, nor is Token Metrics Media LLC registered as an investment adviser or broker-dealer in any jurisdiction.

Information contained herein is not an offer or solicitation to buy, hold, or sell any security. The Token Metrics team has advised and invested in many blockchain companies.

A complete list of their advisory roles and current holdings can be viewed here:

http://tokenmetrics.com/disclosures

THANK YOU!

This book came about as a team effort to fill an educational gap in the crypto investing space. The entire Token Metrics team chipped in to put this book together as an on-ramp for people to learn about investing and deepen their journey to financial empowerment. I want to thank Bill, Forrest, Amisha, Doris, Chase, Brad, my brother Charles, Jad, Zac, Sam, Saurabh, Andy, Paresh, Alejandro, Favour, Zaiying, Jennifer, Ugo, Diego, Dylan, Lali, Daniela, Katheryn, Nina, Dean, and Saira for helping bring this book to life. Even the interns who aren't with us anymore!

This book primarily exists for our customers, who have been requesting a book like this for several years. Now we get to deliver this high-value content to them in the form of a book that stands to become a new investing bible. May this information change your life as radically as it changed mine!

- **Ian Balina**

TABLE OF CONTENTS

———

FOREWORD
BY BEN ARMSTRONG

Let me put it like this, dear reader: I'm jealous of you!

When I first bought Bitcoin, I didn't really know what I was buying. It was 2012 and I needed a specific piece of business software — the guy wanted to be paid in Bitcoin, so I acquired a bunch of Bitcoin without a second thought. It was currency to me, a simple means of exchange for this software. It could've been V-Bucks on Fortnite. It could've been anything at all.

But then the price of this newfangled digital asset shot up, and that little bit in my account became a lot in my account. I smelled an opportunity to cash in, so I used Local Bitcoins to sell my holdings to a stranger in a McDonalds. While I was there connecting to the Wi-Fi, I remember trying to learn more about Bitcoin before completing the sale.

"Maybe instead of getting rid of all this, I should actually figure out what it is," I thought.

There were simply no cohesive educational resources on crypto at the time. I read a GeoCities site that looked like it was from 1994, discussing some Japanese guy named Satoshi. It just didn't connect with me. I was in way over my head and had no idea how to understand it.

Later in 2017, I compared the amount of money I had put into Bitcoin to what that BTC would be worth if I had held onto it. It was quite the seven-figure gap — my lack of crypto understanding in those early days is one of my biggest regrets.

At that point, I just started chasing good content on the topic. I watched YouTube videos, read articles, and generally consumed everything I could about Bitcoin. (Some guy named Ian Balina was already putting out helpful videos at the time!) My own crypto education is a little sloppy because I had no single, consistent source I could turn to for information. But now we come to you in the present day, dear reader!

Suffice it to say that crypto's educational landscape has completely changed. This is perhaps best exemplified by the book you hold in your hands. If I had a unified source of factual information back then about cryptocurrency and how it works, it would've made a significant difference to my overall net worth and life today! So yeah, I'm jealous of you ;-)

The cliché is true: information is power. Conveniently for you, Ian and the Token Metrics team have put together this book to make you more powerful. I hope you use this information to change your life!

INTRODUCTION

———

Hello, my name is Ian Balina! Congratulations on your decision to build a deadly working knowledge of crypto investing — my team and I have been waiting for you!

I'm the founder and CEO of Token Metrics, and to be honest, I'm a little jealous of you right now: the book you're holding contains powerful information that can radically improve your life. By gaining an education on cryptocurrency topics, how the underlying technology works, and how these assets can be profitably traded, you'll not only make yourself richer, but you'll become a beacon of economic empowerment everywhere you go.

The crypto ecosystem is just 12 years young, but the collective market cap of these disparate currencies now exceeds $2 trillion. Cryptocurrency has only grown as an economic force since Satoshi Nakamoto released Bitcoin to the world. Now anyone can use crypto assets to trade their way to financial freedom.

We started Token Metrics with the aim of demystifying what it means to build generational wealth in the 21st century. I know it can work for you because it's already worked for me.

A friend reached out to me while I was working at IBM in 2016, seeking an introduction to IBM's blockchain director. This was unusual to me — why should he care about such a niche branch of technology? He revealed to me that he was a Bitcoin developer who was launching a crypto hedge fund, and that really caught my attention. This guy was my age, yet he saw crypto as an opportunity to make big moves and change lives. I followed his lead from there.

That interaction opened up my eyes. It got me researching crypto and made me into a true believer. I became a regular visitor of news sites-like CoinDesk and Cointelegraph, I read "Digital Gold" by Nathaniel Popper, and after a few months of learning, I went all in on crypto in January 2017.

I started with $20,000. Ethereum was trading between $8-$10, Bitcoin was under $900, and the rest is history — within one year, I turned it into more than $5 million. I furthermore did it in public, logging each trade in a public-facing spreadsheet. At its peak, the spreadsheet was drawing a million unique visitors a month, and I've only gone deeper down the rabbit hole from there.

Crypto changed my life, and now it's my mission to show other people how to do the same thing. This book is your roadmap for going from zero to one in trading crypto. Read it for raw information, sure, but I strongly encourage you to apply the wisdom contained within these pages. It will work as a textbook for anyone, but for true believers, it might just become the bible. The moon is not the limit!

To the moon and beyond!

- Ian Balina

CHAPTER 1

Introduction to Blockchain and Cryptocurrencies

Introduction to Blockchain and Cryptocurrencies

What is a blockchain?

In a word, a blockchain is a database. If you know what we're talking about when we talk about Excel spreadsheets, you're more than halfway to understanding blockchains.

But let's not make the mistake of contextualizing them as something trivial. The reality is quite the opposite: blockchains have a number of technological tricks up their sleeves and hold implications so powerful that they make world governments flinch. These databases may be used for everything from tabulating a vote to tracking the price of crude oil, but the most popular blockchain use case by far is as a decentralized ledger for cryptocurrency transactions.

Blockchain was invented by an unknown individual or group of people working under the pseudonym Satoshi Nakamoto. A technical whitepaper published in 2008 breaks down the whats and whys of blockchain as the software centerpiece that supports Bitcoin (BTC), the world's first blockchain-based cryptocurrency.

Only one blockchain contains all the world's Bitcoin transactions, but every blockchain has the same "special set of skills." Specifically, they are formed on the basis of a decentralized network — it takes a number of independent individuals to work together to perpetuate the network — and data stored in a blockchain is unchangeable.

This means you not only have access to the present value of a "cell" in this database, but you have access to every instance of that cell's previous data. You may also hear this blockchain characteristic called "immutability" or "uncensorability," but it fundamentally means blockchain transactions are impossible to forge.

This is all driven by cryptography. To get an entry-level understanding how cryptography and decentralization make blockchains uncensorable, let's check out this example:

- A new transaction enters the blockchain and generates a hash, a long string of numbers and letters.

- The hash that's generated depends not only on this transaction's characteristics, but on the previous transaction's hash as well.

- Even the smallest of changes in a transaction generates an entirely new hash.

- Nodes, computers responsible for checking the validity of each transaction, inspect hashes to make sure nothing has been forged.

- If most nodes approve a transaction, then that transaction gets written into a block. (In the spreadsheet's analogy to blockchain, this is the moment where data actually enters a cell.)

- Each block then refers to a previous block filled with congruent information, and this chain of blocks forms the so-called blockchain.

Important things to keep in mind about blockchains:

- A blockchain is spread over a network of computers, or nodes. Each computer contains a complete copy of the blockchain.

- A blockchain regularly updates all nodes in its network at a regular interval. For example, the Bitcoin blockchain updates every 10 minutes.

- As soon as a new block is entered, it becomes permanent and cannot be changed. Only new entries can be added to it. The updates occur across all the computers in the network at the same time, making it tough to hack a blockchain.

What is Bitcoin?

Bitcoin launched in January 2009 as the first decentralized cryptocurrency. Without Satoshi Nakamoto to unveil Bitcoin, the cryptocurrency market that we know today simply would not exist.

Bitcoin was conceived as a type of "electronic cash" that allows for sending payments from one party to another, without any financial institutions or central authorities involved. It has become immensely successful in its short history, with a market cap in excess of $1 trillion. Bitcoin's price is often considered the indicator of health for the overall industry.

What is Ethereum?

Ethereum is the most popular alternative cryptocurrency to Bitcoin, but it's also a platform for building and launching uncensorable software applications called dApps. Ethereum has assumed a massive role within the market despite having a market cap that's just a fraction of Bitcoin's.

Ethereum launched in July 2015 and has since become the world's most established, open-ended decentralized software platform.

Ethereum's decentralized software applications are made possible by smart contracts, which are self-executing contracts that represent the terms of an agreement between a buyer and a seller as computer code. Smart contracts running on Ethereum's blockchain are like an autonomous computer that automatically runs a program when specific conditions are met, perhaps buying a set amount of cryptocurrency when that token hits a certain price.

What are altcoins?

The term "altcoin" refers to any cryptocurrency that isn't called Bitcoin or Ethereum. Altcoins generally brand themselves as some improved alternative to Bitcoin, and they vary widely in terms of features and functions.

There are over 6,000 altcoins in existence, and they have names like Litecoin, Algorand, Dogecoin, and beyond.

What are stablecoins?

Stablecoins are the price-steady antidote to volatile cryptocurrencies like BTC. Stablecoins use one of a variety of methods to represent stable value on the blockchain. These are commonly pegged to major fiat assets like the US dollar. Bitcoin may be up today and down tomorrow, but stablecoins exist to capture and preserve value more intuitively.

Why cryptocurrencies are the future

More people than ever are finding fault with the world's centralized fiat financial system. It's perhaps best exemplified in Venezuela: due to the ongoing political and socioeconomic tensions that began in 2016, the country saw 1,370,001% inflation in its national currency in 2019. That kind of number spells out hyperinflation, in which economic circumstances send a currency's value to nearly zero.

Even world superpowers like America stand to benefit here. The financial news cycle nearly flipped upside down in the wake of the GameStop short squeeze, and when retail trading platform Robinhood halted trading on the stock, it was gas on a figurative fire. Despite allying itself and affiliating itself with underdog traders, Robinhood is now the go-to example of how people have way less than 100% control over their money.

And news of the US money printer is hard to keep quiet. With some Americans receiving two rounds of stimulus checks, the masses are more readily connecting the dots that fiat money is less than a fair proposition.

Cryptocurrency technology puts a stop to all of this at once. Blockchains are designed to securely transact value between two parties, whether they trust each other or not. The question that more people are waking up to, however, is about whether they trust the people who print and back their fiat money.

The global financial system

A financial system is a set of institutions that allow for the exchange of funds or currency. These institutions may include banks, insurance companies, and stock exchanges.

A financial system also consists of the rules and practices that borrowers and lenders use to determine economic deals: who gets to finance specific projects, and which projects get funded.

Financial systems exist in varying scales. The smallest may be that of a particular company, the largest is the interconnected global financial system, which covers all financial institutions, borrowers, and lenders in the global economy.

It is the global framework of legal agreements, institutions, and formal and informal economic decision-makers that dictate the international flows of financial capital. The institutions involved in the decision-making end of this system include central banks, major private international banks, government treasuries, monetary authorities, the World Bank, and the International Monetary Fund.

The global financial system comes with a lot of jargon and technical speak, but it all boils down to one straightforward concept: ensuring the stability of the global economy.

That is quite a lot of pressure for the institutions involved, as they are the sole decision-makers and are responsible for the global economy. All it takes is one divergent nation or crisis to shatter this delicate stability.

The evolution of money

Money has been a part of human history for at least 3,000 years. Money's worth comes from it being a medium of exchange, measurement, and store of wealth. If society did not universally agree to this accepted value and form of payment, money would be worthless. That's why money has evolved so drastically over the years.

Coins made from precious metals appeared first, replacing the previous barter system for trading goods and services. Paper currency replaced coins over time as it was more convenient. The first instances of paper currency issued by a government occurred in early North America as shipments between Europe and the colonies took so long that the colonists would often run out of coins. Instead of going back to the barter system, they traded IOUs as a form of currency. In the beginnings of paper currency, it could be traded at any time for precious metal coins at a bank. This standard eventually came to an end in the 20th century and was replaced by fiat money. Fiat is currency used by the government's order and must be accepted as payment. Fiat money is backed by nothing other than the word and power of the issuing government.

Money has continued to evolve in the fiat stage. Most payments are made now without exchanging physical currency — we use plastic cards that point to our money instead, or we use PayPal and Venmo to transact virtually.

The bottom line

Cryptocurrencies are the future as they provide a solution to a rising crisis in the global economy. Cryptocurrencies improve centralized financial systems with their decentralized nature and finite supply.

CHAPTER 2

How to Use and Store Cryptocurrencies

CHAPTER 2

How to Use and Store Cryptocurrencies

Cryptocurrency basics can be confusing. In this guide, we will show you how to buy, send, and receive crypto. We'll also show you where to buy crypto, as well as how to safely store and use it.

How to buy cryptocurrencies

Buying cryptocurrency has become a lot simpler than it used to be. People can purchase cryptocurrencies on cryptocurrency exchanges or on other websites that facilitate the buying and selling of crypto.

Three major types of crypto exchanges

Fiat on-ramps and gateways

The first type of crypto exchange is known as a fiat on-ramp, or fiat gateway. These exchanges accept fiat currencies (paper money) like the US dollar, the euro, the yen, and so on.

Users wire money from their bank account to a fiat on-ramp to buy crypto. Because fiat on-ramps directly deal with fiat currencies, they are subject to lots of regulation. Most regions require financial service businesses to be licensed and regulated.

This translates into strict Know Your Customer (KYC) and Anti Money Laundering (AML) laws. So these exchanges will normally ask for your identification and other personal information to open an account.

Crypto-to-crypto exchanges

The second type of crypto exchange is known as a crypto-to-crypto exchange. These only deal in cryptocurrency for the buying and selling crypto of other cryptos, and they generally support more obscure cryptocurrencies.

An example transaction on this kind of exchange would involve transferring one cryptocurrency from a fiat on-ramp and selling it for another.

Peer-to-peer exchanges

The third type of crypto exchange is known as a peer-to-peer (P2P) exchange. This is about individuals buying directly from other individuals, like a Craigslist for crypto. It also comes with the same risks as buying anything directly from a stranger on Craigslist.

Some P2P exchanges allow for transactions without the two parties ever meeting. This can result in bank wire scams where bad actors cancel transfers after receiving their crypto. We highly advise against using this type of exchange.

An example transaction would involve meeting someone in a safe public place, giving someone physical cash, and receiving cryptocurrency.

Using fiat on-ramps

We strongly recommend using regulated fiat on-ramps. They are easy to use, quick to set up, and safer than any P2P exchange.

Payment methods

Most of these exchanges accept payment by bank transfer or credit card. Some of them also accept PayPal. Each exchange has different levels of regulation, security, and support for different payment methods.

Once your account is set up with KYC and AML, you can start buying cryptocurrency on an exchange. Most exchanges operate like stock-trading platforms: you can buy and hold your cryptocurrency, or exchange it for another cryptocurrency.

Be careful when selecting your cryptocurrency exchange! The crypto industry is riddled with examples of exchanges being hacked, going bankrupt, or otherwise running off with their users' funds. Choose a reputable exchange that's regulated and licensed in your region to mitigate this risk.

Popular fiat on-ramps

Based on a Token Metrics survey, here are the most popular crypto exchanges that our community voted on in our most recent Moon Awards.

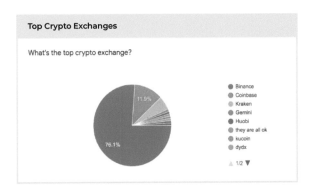

Figure 2.1: Token Metrics Moon Awards: Top Crypto Exchanges

Binance

Binance provides a well-known platform for trading various cryptocurrencies. As of February 2021, Binance was the largest cryptocurrency exchange in the world, with an average daily trading volume over $28.85 billion. Formerly a crypto-to-crypto exchange, Binance has added numerous fiat gateways in over 170 countries.

Coinbase

Coinbase is a digital currency exchange based in San Francisco that launched in June 2012. It's the most prominent American crypto exchange by far. Coinbase supports fiat currencies in approximately 32 countries, as well as crypto transactions and storage for 190 countries worldwide. Coinbase also offers a "pro" version with a cheaper fee structure and more trading options.

Kraken

Kraken is another famous American crypto exchange. It provides cryptocurrency for fiat trading and feeds price information to Bloomberg Terminal. Kraken has one of the most popular over-the-counter (OTC) desks.

How to store, send, and receive crypto

A cryptocurrency wallet is where you store crypto after buying it. Think of it like a bank account: in the same way that you store dollars or euros in a bank account, you store your cryptocurrency in a crypto wallet.

A cryptocurrency wallet is software that stores private and public keys for transacting crypto. It interacts with the blockchain to let users send and receive digital currency and monitor their balance. If you want to use cryptocurrency at all, you will need a digital wallet for it.

Think of a public key as a kind of email address that you share with people who want to send you money. Your private key is like your email password, and it's used to access your wallet and confirm your payments.

Software wallets

There are several types of wallets that provide different ways to store and access your digital currency. Wallets at large can be broken down into three distinct categories: software, hardware, and paper. Software wallets themselves may be desktop, mobile, or online.

Online wallets

Online wallets run in the cloud and are accessible from any connected computing device in any location. While they are more convenient to access, they may also store your private keys online. They are furthermore controlled by a third party, making them more vulnerable to theft and hacking.

Desktop wallets

Desktop wallets run on a desktop or laptop computer, and they are only accessible from that particular device. Desktop wallets offer one of the highest levels of security, but if your computer suffers some security vulnerability, there is always the possibility that you may lose all your funds.

Mobile wallets

Mobile wallets run as a smartphone app. They are usually much simpler than desktop wallets because the best mobile wallets are designed to complement the mobile form factor.

Hardware wallets

Hardware wallets differ from software wallets in that they store a user's private keys on a USB hardware device. Although hardware wallets make transactions online, the funds they contain are stored offline. This delivers increased security.

Hardware wallets can be compatible with several web interfaces, and can support many different cryptocurrencies. Users simply plug in their device to any internet-enabled device, enter a PIN number, send their currency, and confirm the transaction.

Paper wallets

Paper wallets are easy to use and provide a very high level of security. While the term "paper wallet" can simply refer to a physical copy or printout of your public and private keys, it can also refer to a piece of software that generates a pair of keys that are then printed securely.

To transfer cryptocurrency to your paper wallet, simply send funds from your software wallet to the public address shown on your paper wallet.

Alternatively, if you want to withdraw or spend currency, transfer funds from your paper wallet to another wallet's public address. This process, also called "sweeping," can be done manually by entering your private keys, or by scanning the paper wallet's QR code.

Popular crypto wallets

Figure 2.2 shows the top crypto wallets voted on by the Token Metrics community in our most recent Moon Awards.

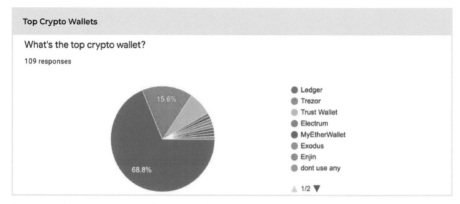

Figure 2.2: Token Metrics Moon Awards: Top Crypto Wallets

Ledger Nano

The Ledger Nano is a hardware wallet that aims to eliminate several attack vectors by using a second security layer. In terms of hardware, the Ledger Wallet Nano is a compact USB device that looks like a portable USB flash drive, except it has buttons for entering a password.

The Ledger Nano supports multiple cryptocurrencies. It can run third-party apps and has Universal 2nd Factor support (U2F) for an additional level of security. You can recover a wallet from a seed phrase without connecting it to a computer!

Trezor

Trezor is a hardware crypto wallet that cannot be infected by malware and never exposes your private keys. Trezor is open source and transparent. It's easy to use, has an intuitive interface, and supports all major operating systems.

Trust Wallet

Trust Wallet is a mobile cryptocurrency wallet owned by Binance. It includes a built-in browser that lets you explore decentralized applications (dApps). dApps are applications that run on blockchains, and the Trust DApp Marketplace can guide you through it. It's an app store that only includes the dApps that meet rigorous quality and security standards.

Use cases for crypto

Most people probably conceive of cryptocurrencies as a high-risk investment for millennials and the tech elite. There's so much more under the surface.

Low-cost money transfers

The most straightforward use case for crypto is to quickly and cheaply send and receive payments. Money transfers that go the legacy finance route have higher fees and take three to five business days to process — sometimes even longer. The low transaction fees associated with digital currencies like Litecoin (LTC), Stellar (XLM), or Bitcoin Cash (BCH) make them excellent payment systems for international money transfers.

Store of value

Bank accounts get frozen more often than people realize, especially in jurisdictions with a dubious rule of law. When it happens, people can find themselves with little or no access to cash, even if they've done nothing wrong.

This is where one of the most powerful uses for cryptocurrency comes into play. Cryptocurrencies are censorship-resistant and can't be shut down.

They function as an alternative store of wealth that only the individuals with the wallet's private keys can gain access to. No authority can freeze a Bitcoin transaction.

Investing

Anyone with an internet connection can become an investor in innovative early-stage tech startups while simultaneously providing those ventures with much-needed capital. Access to these deals in the past would have only been available to experienced venture capitalists and accredited investors. But the advent of cryptocurrency has opened the floodgates to anyone who wants to participate.

Privacy

Privacy-centric digital currencies such as Monero (XMR), Zcash (ZEC), and PIVX (PIVX) let users make their financial transactions anonymously. That means individuals can make money transfers without any explanation to banks or governments.

Non-cash remittances

The Nigerian blockchain startup SureRemit, for example, lets its users send non-cash remittances from anywhere in the world to select African nations. African diaspora around the world can purchase SureRemit's native RMT tokens, which are then used within the SureRemit app to make non-cash remittances for things like mobile data top-ups or utility bill payments for families in Africa.

Incentivized rewards and payments

Steemit, the world's first incentivized social media and blogging platform, lets publishers receive financial rewards for their work. These rewards come in the form of cryptocurrency for posting and curating content on the network. Operating similarly to Reddit and Medium, Steemit financially empowers its users by rewarding them for contributing to the platform, as opposed to selling user data to third parties. This has made Steemit particularly popular in emerging markets. Decentralized blockchain-based cloud storage solutions like Storj let users earn cryptocurrency in exchange for renting out their hard drive space to others on a peer-to-peer basis. Storj and other decentralized cloud storage solutions, like Siacoin and Filecoin, provide a cheaper and more secure alternative to existing corporate cloud storage platforms while giving users a new revenue stream.

Travel

It is now possible to travel the world by spending crypto. Established travel agents like CheapAir and Destinia accept Bitcoin as a payment method for booking flights, car rentals, and hotels. The growth of the world's Bitcoin ATM market also means travelers can now easily convert their cryptocurrency into local currency in most major cities around the world.

Payments

Richard Branson's commercial space travel company Virgin Galactic announced in November 2013 that it will accept Bitcoin payments for space travel bookings. While the California-based company has not successfully launched a commercial space flight, several future astronauts have already paid for their $250,000 tickets in Bitcoin, including crypto advocates Cameron and Tyler Winklevoss.

Shopping

Last but not least, you can also use your cryptocurrency to buy a Lamborghini. The Bitcoin luxury marketplace De Louvois enables the "crypto rich" to purchase sports cars. It also offers a range of other luxury goods like art, fine wines, and real estate for those with deep digital pockets.

The bottom line

Crypto works for low-cost money transfers, as a store of value, as an investment opportunity, a privacy tool, and more. Securing your crypto is vital since transactions are permanent. You should never share your private key with anyone, as you could get hacked and lose all your money. If you lose your private key, you will no longer have access to your crypto.

CHAPTER 3

Securing Your Crypto from Hackers

Securing Your Crypto
from Hackers

The breakout popularity of Bitcoin and Ethereum has made virtual currencies a new target for hackers. Protecting your crypto assets is an essential part of being a crypto investor. When a cryptocurrency account gets compromised, it can easily spell disaster.

There are numerous reports of traders and investors who got hacked by way of phishing scams, exchange scams, improper private key management, and more. The crypto paradigm calls for you to be your own bank, so we need to discuss how to protect your assets in this brave new crypto world.

Exchange hacks

Perhaps the most notorious exchange hack was Mt. Gox in 2014. It cost users 850,000 Bitcoins, equivalent to more than $7 billion today. Exchange hacks can happen a few different ways: an insider might go rogue, or a portion of secret keys gets removed.

Who better to exploit an exchange's security than an insider who works there? They can merge chunks of old and new keys, essentially locking the exchange out of its funds. An attacker can leverage flaws in the essential management process in software libraries. The attacker can then exploit the relationship between the exchange and its customer and create false validation statements.

Exchanges can also get hacked when trusted parties are denied their portion of the keys. When this is the case, a malicious party could send out messages that would essentially allow them to assign these values, letting them use the information and extract funds.

For your own crypto dealings, you should use an end-to-end encrypted email that's entirely separate from your primary address. Avoid connecting it with anything pertaining to your work or personal life in order to decrease your chances of becoming a target. An end-to-end encrypted email provider is vital because it keeps all communications encrypted and out of sight of third parties, even the email provider itself. Now that's protection!

Protonmail and Tutanota are two popular end-to-end encrypted email providers. Registering with either of them could help keep your personal information safe and protect your funds from being stolen.

Two-factor authentication furthermore adds on an extra layer of security to everything. It requires a second device to authenticate your login and add security. Two-factor authentication is also great for protecting yourself outside of crypto — use it for your regular email, banking, and social media.

Standard two-factor authentication apps include Google Authenticator, Authy, Microsoft Authenticator, and Duo Mobile. They also work offline. You could also purchase a universal second factor like a Google Titan Security Key or a Yubikey. These are physical security keys that can easily be attached to a keychain.

Avoid two-factor authentication by SMS. Hackers are known to steal phone numbers via SIM swap attacks by purchasing illegal employee access to carrier support accounts or even blackmailing phone carrier staff for insider access. This provides them direct access to port your telephone number to their own phone, receiving your SMS verification codes directly for log-in access.

Phishing attacks

Phishing attacks work to obtain private information like bank accounts and credit card numbers by presenting themselves as a normal and trustworthy procedure. Attackers can use texts, emails, or websites that appear legitimate, but then make you install an application or enter in a password that could give an attacker free and unlimited access to your device.

Hackers may even clone popular websites like Twitter, subtly changing the domain name to "tw1tter.com" on the premise that no one would notice, and would enter their true login details. Check URLs carefully!

The use of a secure domain name system (DNS), such as Quad 9, helps filter out malicious domains and links, and could provide a basic level of phishing protection. DNS services translate domain names to IP addresses, therefore humans do not need to memorize legitimate and illegitimate IP addresses.

Installing the Adblock browser extension to cancel pop-ups and ads from appearing can offer another layer of protection from shady websites.

Script blockers like Privacy Badger stop suspicious computer code from executing and prevent tracking from different sites.

The bottom line is that the best way to defend against phishing hacks is to avoid clicking links to websites that are unfamiliar or otherwise seem dodgy. And definitely don't enter your account information anywhere except the secure website pertaining to that account.

Social engineering

Social engineering is a type of cyber attack closely related to phishing: attackers exploit human psychology to gain private information, manipulating victims into revealing their information.

This attack is most effective against people with a general lack of internet awareness, primarily young children and the elderly. These attacks could take place over the phone, through the computer, or even in person. The attackers often masquerade as someone who requires desperate help, exploiting people's kindness. Victims may be manipulated into installing malware that lets the attacker access their computer.

There are multiple methods for protecting yourself against social engineering scams.

- Employees at corporations could go through training to prevent situations like the data breach Target experienced in 2013.

- Make sure the answers to your personal security questions can't be found online.

- Operations security practices can limit the amount of information that's obtainable.

- Be wary of third-party vendors that hold large volumes of data for multiple companies. This is a goldmine for social engineers.

- Carry out adequate risk assessments to prevent leaks.

On July 15th, 2020, Twitter suffered a major social engineering hack. Hackers leveraged connections to breach Twitter's system and access verified accounts belonging to Barack Obama, Elon Musk, Kanye West, and many more. The hackers tweeted as these public figures, giving out an address for receiving Bitcoin and claiming that any amount received there would be doubled and sent back. The hackers collected more than $100,000 with this scam and caused panic at Twitter as all verified accounts were temporarily prevented from tweeting.

Network hacks

As mentioned earlier, it's best to use a VPN on public internet connections. Otherwise anyone can listen in on what you're doing, and in some cases they can even receive your data in plain text.

Shodan.io is one popular tool for hackers. It works like a search engine for internet devices.

A hacker can enter an IP address and the tool will show them the types of equipment and information needed for finding vulnerabilities. This makes it possible for bad actors to compile a list of IP addresses that don't have protection, and then attack them.

Hardware firewalls are an important component of your security. They integrate directly with your internet connection to filter out malicious traffic and pass clean data to your router. They're stronger than software firewalls because they aren't limited to protecting one device, but any device that connects to your network.

Good hardware firewalls include Firewalla Red, Ubiquiti, Protectli, and Netgate. Get a firewall with Deep Packet Inspection (DPI). DPI checks the actual packets being sent from the internet to your router and inspects them for malware or viruses.

Phone hacks (SIM swaps)

SIM swaps are perhaps the most common type of phone hack. They mislead your phone provider into sending your secure data to them instead of you.

A prominent SIM swap case saw Michael Terpin lose $23.8 million in 2019. His hacker, Nicholas Truglia, managed to perform SIM swaps on eight other people, including his father.

If a SIM swap has occurred, you'll immediately lose the ability to send, receive messages and make phone calls. Sudden loss of phone service or connectivity could be a sign of a phone hack, so the best possible move would be to call your provider from a different phone.

Other security precautions

Backup

Backup your wallet early and often. Regular backups can protect your cryptocurrency in case of a computer failure. Be sure to backup all the wallet.dat files, and store that backup at multiple secure locations — put it on a USB drive, store it on an external hard drive, burn it to a CD, and so on.

A great encrypted USB drive is the Apricorn Aegis Secure Key, which requires a physical PIN entry on the device itself before it can be used with a computer.

Software updates

Make sure you keep your applications up to date and run the latest versions. A wallet running on old software can be an easy target for hackers. The latest version will have a better security system in place and increase the security of your crypto holdings.

Multi-signature

The concept of multi-signature security is gaining popularity. It involves approval from multiple people before a transaction can take place. This reduces the threat of theft, as one person alone can't make any transactions.

Whitelisting commonly used wallet addresses

If you commonly transfer crypto from your exchange account to a Nano Ledger wallet then you can whitelist your Nano Ledger addresses. If your account were ever compromised, the attacker would have to go through additional verification to add a new wallet address for withdrawal. This is typically done by email or two-factor authentication verification.

The bottom line

The crypto industry is continuously evolving, so it's important to update yourself on the latest security news, hacking techniques, and the countermeasures to prevent them. Remember: you are your own bank, so the safety of your finances is up to you.

CHAPTER 4

Introduction to Value Investing

CHAPTER 4

Introduction to Value Investing

Value investing and the concept of a benchmark

Value investors are those looking to buy high-quality assets when they are cheap. But what does "cheap" even mean? To answer that, we must discuss the idea of a benchmark.

A benchmark is merely a reference point. In equities, a benchmark is usually a price-earnings (PE) ratio. PEs are numbers that typically range between 5 and 100. The specific calculation is the price per share divided by estimated earnings per share two years from now.

Let's start with a famous stock index: the S&P 500, or SPX. The aggregate price-earnings ratio of all the companies in the SPX is around 23. Any stock with a price-earnings ratio below 23 is considered "cheaper than the market."

A stock with a PE of 10 or 12 might be described as a value stock because it is much cheaper than the market. But just because a stock has a lower PE than the market doesn't make it a good investment. It could be a public utility company that grows revenue and earnings at a much slower rate.

On the other hand, if a stock has a PE ratio higher than SPX, it could be considered expensive. Again, "expensive" doesn't necessarily mean you should avoid the stock. Companies with high PE ratios often have strong growth prospects. Most big tech companies have PE ratios above their benchmarks.

The point here is that value investing has its own jargon, and it centers around whether an asset seems cheap or expensive. That can be compared to a benchmark like an index or the historical range for the stock's PE.

When do famous value investors buy and sell?

As you might suspect, value investors look to buy when a high-quality asset is cheap, and they endeavor to sell if the asset changes in character and becomes expensive. Value investors like Warren Buffet frequently make significant purchases of cheap assets during times of crisis or recession. One example saw Warren Buffet buy Goldman Sachs stock in the wake of the 2008 recession. Buffet was effectively lending money to Goldman at a rate of 9% when interest rates were (at the time) 0%. Buffet took advantage of the hysteria in financial markets to invest in a high-quality company when others were panicking and shunning such assets.

Conversely, value investors sell during bubble phases. They sell when valuations are so elevated that they don't make sense. In this day and age, nobody would question an investment in Amazon (AMZN), but back in 2000 when Amazon was just an online bookstore, its valuation reached an extreme. The valuation was so high relative to earnings that one analyst did a famous calculation determining that Amazon would have to sell every book in the world 1.1 times to justify its stock price.

Statistics like that indicated that the tech sector was overvalued, creating a bubble waiting to pop. When you hear talk that a long-term rally justifies super-high valuations because "this time is different" or there is a "new paradigm" or "new economy" developing, that can frequently indicate a selling opportunity.

To be a value investor, you have to have some metrics to determine whether an instrument is cheap or expensive. It could be something as complex as a PE ratio, but it could also be as simple as a back-of-the-envelope calculation.

Value investing in Bitcoin

There is no textbook for determining if Bitcoin is cheap or expensive. At Token Metrics, the measure we have used effectively is the Bitcoin dominance statistic. We believe it is crypto's version of the PE ratio.

Bitcoin dominance measures the percentage that Bitcoin takes up when looking at the total crypto market cap. At the top of the market in 2017, when Bitcoin was near $20,000, it occupied roughly 85% of the overall market cap. This means Bitcoin was outright expensive compared to the rest of the crypto market.

Fast-forward to early 2019, and Bitcoin was trading below $4,000. Bitcoin dominance had shrunk to nearly 30%. In this case, Bitcoin was obviously on sale at discount prices, but given its volatility, our ranges for "cheap" and "expensive" are changing with the times. We are currently using 65% as the pivot for costly or cheap: at 65%, Bitcoin seems costly.

Our twist, however, is that when we see Bitcoin as "expensive," it's a great time to buy altcoins. Eyeballing the chart, if Bitcoin dominance ever fell near 40%, then we can assume Bitcoin is cheap and it could set up a Bitcoin price rally.

Here's the bottom line: when doing value investing, you want to keep it simple. Warren Buffet has teams that run numbers, but his decision-making process often seems qualitative and straightforward. While there is no perfect metric for "cheap" or "expensive," we think you can be creative. Invent your own metric or combination of parameters. We hope, however, that we gave you a start.

Value investing in altcoins

Value investing in crypto is vastly different from value investing in the stock market. Normal data points like company financials are just not available in crypto.

Investing in crypto is similar to angel investing and venture capital due to the lack of public company data. There is no regulatory body like the Securities and Exchange Commission that publicly forces crypto companies to publish their financials or metrics.

What makes this even more complicated is that crypto companies are tradable on crypto exchanges. It essentially combines venture capital startups with public capital markets. Add to the equation that crypto is a global market open 24 hours a day, seven days a week, and we are now presented with the Wild West of investing.

Despite this, there is a certain order to the chaos. Consistent strategies are available for finding undervalued projects. Rather than reading quarterly and annual reports, crypto investors read whitepapers. These are generally technical papers describing the technology behind a cryptocurrency. Crypto investors also look for large and passionate communities of users, all-star teams, reputable early venture capital firms supporting the project, consistent traction, and execution on roadmap milestones.

A simple model for value investing in crypto is to find projects with long-term staying power that have a low market capitalization relative to their competition. For example, if you find a new but relatively unknown cryptocurrency project with a market cap of $5 million, you should compare it to its peers. If you discover during your research that this project has better technology and more traction than its competitors, who have an average market cap of $500 million, you might just be onto a hidden gem. You essentially want to find low-cap cryptocurrencies with solid fundamentals and technology that have the potential to blossom into the next large-cap cryptocurrency.

The bottom line

Value investing calls for you to be a contrarian by definition. Value investors buy when everyone else is selling, and they sell when everyone else is buying. The strategy is simple, but sticking to it and going against the market for the rest of your life is hard.

CHAPTER 5

Introduction to Risk Management

Introduction to Risk Management

Warren Buffet is famous for stating that the number one rule of investing is not to lose money. He's also famous for saying the number two rule of investing is not to forget rule number one. Risk management is vital for all investors and traders. It is far easier to lose money than it is to make money, especially in crypto. As a result, having a good risk management foundation goes a long way towards becoming an intelligent investor and trader.

What is risk?

Risk is the chance that the actual gains from an outcome will differ from the estimated expected outcome. In finance, it refers to the degree of uncertainty or loss inherent in an investment decision. This relationship between risk and return is a fundamental idea in finance. The greater the risk an investor is willing to take, the greater the return potential.

This concept is also known as "risk tolerance," or the level of risk an investor is willing to have associated with an investment. Specific factors like age, personality, experience, income, and more comprise an investor's risk profile and indicate the level of risk that one will tolerate.

Different types of risk

There are five types of risks within financial markets: business risk, credit or default risk, country risk, liquidity risk, and market risk. While specific risk measures are more common than others, they all are worthy of exploration as they influence investor decisions across the spectrum.

Business risk

Business risk refers to the essential ability of a business to function successfully. To that effect, this type of risk associates with practical questions that business analysts face daily, such as whether the company is bringing in enough revenue to generate profit. Businesses usually require a variety of operations to survive, including (but not limited to) salaries, production costs, facility rent, office, and administrative expenses.

In addition to these face-value costs, also known as "sunk costs," businesses take on additional risks known as exposure. This measure of risk is related to potential future loss resulting from a specific activity or event. Businesses typically engage in a risk management strategy known as Enterprise Risk Management (ERM) to protect themselves from risk exposure. ERM is a plan-based business strategy that aims to identify, assess, and prepare for any dangers, hazards, and other potentials for disaster that may interfere with the operations and objectives of the business.

Credit risk

Credit risk, or default risk, refers to the financial loss that a party will incur if the counterparty to a transaction fails to fulfill its financial obligations in a timely manner. Credit risk can be measured with "the Five Cs": credit history, capacity to repay, capital, loan conditions, and associated collateral. Credit history is one of the most important metrics, as one's credit score can directly impact their ability to make purchases. Individuals with a bad credit history pose higher credit risk and therefore have to pay a higher interest rate to provide a security measure for all parties in a transaction.

Country risk

Country risk refers to a situation where a country defaults on its financial commitments to one or more countries. This type of risk has vast implications for the international economy. When a country defaults, it immediately impacts the exchange rates between nations. When investors predict a change in future financial conditions, they will alter their current investment decisions. But when such market shocks happen without warning, they drastically affect net exports, resulting in an unexpected appreciation or depreciation of foreign currencies. There are two independent sub-studies of risk within country risk: foreign exchange risk and interest rate risk. People commonly confuse foreign exchange rates and interest rates. These two measures do tend to move in the same direction, but this is not always true — some conditions impact volatility in both rates differently.

Country risk is impacted by three factors: economic risk, political risk, and sovereign risk. Economic risk refers to the ability of a country to pay back its debts. (One should note that there is a difference between a country's ability to repay debts and the country's documented history). Many large economies like the United States have accumulated massive debt with little intention of repayment soon. The ability to repay comes from a stable and robust economy, and the ability to raise and collect taxes. Political risk refers to the political conditions within a country. Since the political climate is closely tied with the performance of a country's currency, investors need to be aware of global headlines.

Monetary policy risk refers to the uncertainty that a foreign central bank will, without warning, alter its foreign exchange regulations. Such action by the central bank can significantly affect currency value. This manner of decision-making is unattractive to investors and therefore disincentivizes investment in such countries.

Liquidity risk

Liquidity risk refers to when a company or other financial institution is unable to meet short-term financial demands. Since liquidity is the ease with which an asset can be converted to cash, an institution's liquidity plays a significant role in short horizons. But the inability of a company to meet its short-term demands doesn't mean it has no money left. Firms often allocate a majority of their money into long-term securities that have a higher payout rather than hold cash for investment purposes. The problem with this is that converting hard long-term assets into cash is time-consuming and capital-intensive at the same time.

There are two types of liquidity risk: cash flow risk and product risk. Cash flow risk is the extent that future cash flows may fall short of investor expectations. This situation would arise as a response to changes in several market variables. Product risk (also called asset risk) is the default potential of a particular asset in response to market value fluctuations. Both types of liquidity risk are relatively niched, so investors won't typically combat threats against them individually, but rather against liquidity risk.

Market risk

Market risk is the potential for the value of an investment to decrease due to changes in market factors that drive prices. These factors impact the overall performance of financial markets and can only be reduced by diversifying with assets that aren't correlated with the market.

Market risk is sometimes called "systematic risk" because it relates to factors that impact the entire market, like a recession. The risk of losses on financial investments is primarily caused by adverse price movements. Market risk contrasts with specific risk, also known as business risk or unsystematic risk, tied directly with a market sector or the performance of a particular asset.

Risks in crypto

Ever since Satoshi Nakamoto invented Bitcoin, it and other cryptocurrencies have been met with investor skepticism. The general opinion from financial professionals is that there is a minimal guarantee of profitability in Bitcoin investments, and inexperienced investors should only invest money that they are willing to lose.

While some of this hesitancy is valid, it is still worth exploring why critics believe cryptocurrency is one of the riskiest assets in financial markets. The first reason is that cryptocurrency is an entirely new field of finance, so any problems it runs into are altogether unprecedented. But the issue is that investors cannot permanently alter their expectations in advance enough to hedge their investments. Cryptocurrencies were initially very volatile because early investors could not easily short them. The launch of options and futures has allowed more investors to short cryptocurrencies, resulting in more stable prices. In other words, the more liquid the asset becomes, the less volatile it is.

Due to a lack of trust in cryptocurrency's functionality, many individuals engage with crypto only after a thorough understanding of the product. Crypto has additionally attracted a large number of hackers and bad actors. Given this industry's entirely virtual platform, hackers have broken into exchanges and infected individual computers with malware that steals crypto. Forcing investors to rely on the strength of their computer security systems is too large of a risk to take for many that have many other investment opportunities available.

Price variability causes crypto's fluctuations in value to be entirely unpredictable. This adds to crypto's riskiness. There is a theoretically unlimited supply of money produced through a central bank in the fiat currency world. Due to the limited availability, cryptocurrencies can appear to be more volatile than other conventional currencies.

The lack of a comprehensive and unified system to regulate the distribution and use of cryptocurrencies only adds to the risk of holding. Additionally, there could exist many potential compliance risks that come with holding crypto.

Managing and hedging risk

While investors take varying levels of risk, people prefer to hedge or minimize their risk as much as possible. Risk management is forecasting, evaluating financial risks, and identifying procedures to avoid or reduce their impact. The two factors that most influence risk management are the time horizon and the liquidity of investments.

Time horizon has an indirect relationship with risk and volatility: the longer the investment horizon, the lower the risk level, and thus the higher the potential returns. Long-term investors are in a position to allocate a substantial portion of their investment portfolios to higher-risk investments than short-term investors.

An investment's liquidity also has an indirect relationship with risk. If an investment isn't liquid, it can't be sold quickly. This is harmful to investors who quickly need to get rid of a particular asset.

But despite the risk in the crypto market, those keen enough will learn ways to reduce risk. Risk management tools like stop-losses and strategies like hedging come in handy. Hedging Bitcoin, or any cryptocurrency for that matter, involves strategically opening trades so that a gain or loss in one position is offset by changes to the other position's value.

Generally speaking, if you're concerned about your risk, it is probably safer to reduce your position size or close your position altogether. But hedging is a valuable strategy for traders who want to maintain their original crypto holding but create a neutral exposure.

With the rise of stablecoins and decentralized finance, we can see that the ability to lend your crypto and receive interest on it is becoming a very prominent way to dilute your risk. (This is referred to as yield farming). There are many ways to hedge risks in traditional finance, like options contracts or risk-free rate assets such as government bonds. In crypto, stablecoins have low volatility that makes them less risky than other cryptocurrencies. They are commonly backed by, or pegged to, a reserve asset like gold or the US dollar. But even if they seem to have no exchange rate risk, they introduce counterparty risks.

One example is Tether. Despite being pegged to the dollar, it once lost 15% of its value against the dollar. Such coins rely on a central authority's permission to exist, which flies in the face of crypto's decentralization thesis.

Consider an example where US regulators would ban USD-backed crypto assets. This introduces new risks instead of diluting the overall portfolio risk. Therefore, holding a stablecoin is not always enough to diversify and manage risk: investors should also diversify their stablecoin holdings.

How to measure risk

All risk, including financial risk, is measured by calculating the amount of volatility or the difference between actual returns and expected returns. In mathematical terms, this difference is called the standard deviation. The standard deviation has a direct relationship with volatility, and by extension, risk.

If a financial instrument has a high standard deviation, then it is correlated with a high level of risk, and vice versa. Though several statistical measures are used to calculate risk, the standard deviation is the most common one out of simplicity.

It is essential to note that standard deviation accounts for not just downside volatility, but upside volatility as well. Investors usually care about downside volatility more than upside volatility, so there are other risk metrics besides the standard deviation. One includes downside deviation, which only considers the volatility of negative returns.

Furthermore, the standard deviation works best for normal distributions. So when the distribution of returns is not normally distributed, this measure is not very helpful. The critical point to understand is that risk management is more art than science, so there is no single metric that can wholly encompass a portfolio's riskiness. It is better to use multiple metrics to get better insights.

Quantitative risk management models

Quantitative risk management frameworks must be able to identify, quantify, and mitigate risks. There are various sources of risk in crypto, and thus there are multiple methods and metrics that help investors manage their portfolio risk. Here we will introduce basic concepts and techniques for quantitative risk management.

Risk factors and loss distribution

Buckle up, things are about to get technical! It is productive to compute a Loss Distribution function to understand and measure your risk exposure. The loss distribution function is simply the change in your portfolio value over your time horizon. Since the future value of your portfolio is unobservable today, it is random, and thus the loss distribution is a probability distribution.

Following standard risk management practices, the value of the portfolio is modeled by risk factors, and accordingly, the loss distribution is modeled by the changes in risk factors. By analyzing the differences in risk factors, you can compute the mean and variance of the loss distribution to manage portfolio risk better.

Risk measures based on loss distributions

Working with loss distributions is meaningful since the distribution contains all statistical information about possible losses. Many risk measures like value-at-risk (VaR) and conditional value-at-risk (CVaR) are based on the loss distribution of portfolios. VaR is defined as the maximum amount expected to be lost over a given time horizon and at a predefined confidence level. For example, a 95% one-month VaR of $100,000 means that over the next month, there is 95% confidence that the maximum loss is $100,000. The best way to compute VaR is through Monte-Carlo simulations that we will discuss later.

However, it is essential to note some shortcomings of VaR, like a high sensitivity to estimation errors. Conditional value-at-risk is defined as the expected loss that is incurred if VaR is exceeded. It therefore "looks further into the tail" of the distribution. For risk management purposes, it is crucial to keep an eye on both two measures.

Factor models

Factor models are widely used in finance. The most prominent are the one-factor model of asset returns, the Capital Asset Pricing Model (CAPM), and the Fama-French Three-Factor model. It relates the returns on one asset to multiple predictive factors that could be statistical, macroeconomic, or fundamentals.

For example, consider this Three-Factor model for a crypto portfolio:

- Market Factor – The value-weighted return of the underlying cryptocurrency.

- Size Factor – The spread between the largest and smallest cryptocurrencies by market cap.

- Momentum Factor – The difference between high momentum and low momentum cryptocurrencies.

Factor models effectively analyze portfolio risk exposure, decompose the risk of a portfolio into various factors, and quantify how much each factor contributes to the portfolio's risk.

Scenario analysis, or "stress tests"

Scenario-based risk management is vital, as it allows investors to test their portfolios' performance in different scenarios. Each scenario assumes that the various risk factors of the portfolio have moved by some fixed amount. For example, you could invent scenarios like "Alt Season," "Bitcoin Dominance," "Crypto Market Crash," "Mount Gox Crypto Exchange Hack" and see how your portfolio performed in each scenario.

In this case, we don't need to calculate a probability distribution, so it is a relatively simple procedure. While scenario tables are a valuable source of information, there are potential drawbacks as well, like the difficulty in identifying risk factors and determining a "reasonable" shift in these risk factors.

Monte-Carlo simulation

The Monte-Carlo simulation method lets the investor see all the possible outcomes of their investment portfolio and their probability of occurring, allowing for better decision-making given all the uncertainty.

The Monte-Carlo simulation performs risk analysis by building models of possible results, substituting a range of values using a probability distribution for any inherent uncertainty factor. It then calculates re-sults repeatedly, each time with a different set of random values from the probability functions. Depending upon the number of uncertain outcomes and the ranges specified for them, a Monte-Carlo simulation could involve thousands of recalculations before it is complete.

Monte-Carlo simulations produce distributions of possible outcome values. By using probability distributions, variables can have different probabilities of different outcomes occurring. Probability distributions are a much more realistic way of describing uncertainty in variables of a risk analysis.

Using Monte-Carlo simulations allows the investor to see how their portfolio will perform in hundreds of different scenarios. This will give them insights into both the "average" of all possible outcomes and the extreme case scenarios.

Tail risk management

The tail of a loss distribution refers to so-called black swan events, an unpredictable occurrence that goes far beyond the market norm. These are very rare and very far from the mean. Distributions with light tails, like a normal distribution, assume that outliers are extremely rare, and distributions with fat tails associate a higher probability of extreme out-comes. It is essential to understand the tail of the loss distribution at hand, as one loss that seems impossible could occur and wipe out your entire portfolio. Given that tail events are infrequent and hard to predict, risk management procedures need to take them into account and not to be too exposed to such events.

Model risk

When using a quantitative model to allocate capital, it is essential to understand the model's risks. Using a quantitative model as a "black box" could be fatal if you don't know how the model works and why it recommends specific actions.

For instance, consider a simple mean-variance optimization model that allows investors to achieve an efficient portfolio, a portfolio with the highest expected return for a target level of risk, or a portfolio with the least risk for the expected return. The model will give the optimal asset allocation amount to each asset in the portfolio. This model is susceptible to estimation errors in expected returns and covariances. It could produce extreme portfolios composed of extreme shorts and excessive longs, giving an illusion of diversification.

Another problem is that the allocation could change drastically for a minimal change in the inputs. Therefore, any investor using quantitative models should understand the inherent risks in the model to know when to trust it fully and when to be skeptical.

The bottom line

Risk is the chance that the actual gains from an outcome will differ from the estimated expected outcome. In finance, it refers to the degree of uncertainty or loss inherent in an investment decision. Risk management is more of an art than science, so there is no single metric that can wholly encompass a portfolio's riskiness.

CHAPTER 6

Building a Portfolio

CHAPTER 6

Building a Portfolio

Portfolio asset allocation

Before determining the asset allocation, investors need to determine their investment objectives and the degree of risk they want to bear. One needs to know how much energy they can spend on the investment, how much money they can allocate toward investing, and how much money they need to achieve their investment goals.

Identifying your investment goals and degree of risk will help you determine your investment strategy with short-term or long-term investments. This critical distinction is highlighted in the Token Metrics platform: you can change your analyses and ratings from short-term trader to long-term value-investor. Building a portfolio for short-term gains is very different from a portfolio built for a long-term strategy.

Strategic asset allocation

Strategic asset allocation is better suited for long-term investing goals. Here, the allocation to different assets in your portfolio is based on your goals and risk profile, regardless of the market's current state. The key point is that your allocation only changes when your goals or risk profile change. It is purely internal and doesn't account for macroeconomic factors.

Tactical asset allocation

Tactical asset allocation is better suited for short-term trading. In this case, your allocation often changes to take advantage of potentially profitable opportunities in the market. It is vital to understand market dynamics and transaction costs, as frequent rebalancing is required to generate profit.

Three basic portfolios

There are three types of portfolios: aggressive, balanced, and conservative.

Aggressive portfolio

An aggressive investor pursues an investment with high returns. However, higher returns typically mean higher risks. An aggressive investor must be willing to bear more risk in exchange for higher returns. Investing rarely involves free lunches or riskless investments.

Conservative portfolio

For a conservative investor, the risk they bear is minimal. Consequently, such investors typically obtain stable and low returns.

Balanced portfolio

A balanced portfolio is simply a portfolio blended between a conservative and aggressive style. This is the most common investment style.

In equities, portfolio styles are typically determined by the number of years remaining until retirement. For example, a new investor in their twenties with no kids typically has an aggressive portfolio strategy. The idea is that if their portfolio was to lose money, they have more years to recover their investment.

A balanced portfolio strategy might be suitable for someone in their forties with a family to support. This investor has dependents and less time to bounce back from any failed investments. They may have obligations such as a mortgage, loans, and college savings.

With a conservative portfolio strategy, this investor is typically close to retirement age and has been investing for decades. Being on the home stretch, they have already gone through the aggressive and balanced portfolio phases. They've made their money and now are more concerned with not losing it before they retire.

Building a crypto portfolio

Once a portfolio style is determined, capital must now be allocated to the appropriate asset classes. At this moment, we need to choose under-priced assets based on factors such as fundamentals, technology, technical analysis, and performance metrics to diversify our portfolios.

We understand that many investors do not have time to do in-depth analysis on hundreds of cryptocurrencies. This is why we built Token Metrics.

How to diversify your portfolio

The old adage is true: investors should not put all their eggs in one basket. This is what diversification is all about — it's essential in building your portfolio. To achieve a diversified portfolio, investors must buy asset classes with the minimum correlation between each other.

In essence, if one asset in your portfolio moves down, you want another asset to compensate for that by moving up. Diversification works very quickly. When adding an uncorrelated asset to your portfolio, the marginal contribution of this asset to your portfolio is very high at first. It then slows down as you add more assets. Diversification can sometimes be an illusion too. Correlations can change over time, and in periods of market stress, the correlation between assets increases drastically.

This is because everyone is trying to sell the same popular assets in a market crash. So even if your portfolio seems properly diversified for equilibrium market conditions, it could change drastically when markets are stressed. A flight-to-liquidity is a financial market phenomenon that happens when investors sell what they perceive to be less liquid or higher risk investments and buy more liquid and safer assets, such as US treasuries, stablecoins, or cash.

Portfolio construction and risk allocation

Exposure to specific cryptocurrencies depends mainly on your risk appetite. This can be simply defined as your ability to take risks. Stocks have higher risks than bonds, but stocks can also provide higher returns due to the risk-return trade-off. Conversely, bonds are often safer than stocks, but bonds have lower returns as time passes. The combination of the two helps create a balanced portfolio.

For example, if your risk tolerance is balanced in the global market, then a young person's typical portfolio will contain 50% stocks and 50% bonds. We can draw some similarities between the traditional and cryptocurrency markets if we apply these measures.

Some think investing in Bitcoin is less risky than investing in altcoins. Using this, we can adjust our risk exposure to suit our tolerance. For example, a risky portfolio might consist of 80% altcoins and 20% Bitcoin. At the same time, a safe portfolio might have 90% Bitcoin and 10% altcoins.

To sum it up, ask yourself where you are on the risk-reward spectrum. Before continuing, we must note the following: the basic assumption we are making is that the cryptocurrency market will grow over time.

Therefore, the cryptocurrency portfolio should be measured in Bitcoin rather than dollars, as our investment hypothesis is that fiat currencies will decrease in value versus Bitcoin over the long term. This results from quantitative easing by central banks, inflation, and Bitcoin being a scarce asset.

Blue chip assets

In most crypto portfolios, you will hold Bitcoin or Ethereum. These are the blue chip cryptocurrencies. Think of these as the Dow Jones of crypto, the most reputable and mature cryptocurrencies.

Large-cap, mid-cap, and low-cap assets

Diversifying sometimes means selecting varying cryptocurrencies based on their market cap. Cryptocurrencies within the top 20 market cap are considered large-cap cryptos. Those between the top 20 and top 100 are typically considered mid-cap cryptos. Those outside the top 100 market cap are considered low-cap cryptos.

As the market grows and changes, cryptocurrencies can shift across these categories. A diverse portfolio will have a combination of large-cap, mid-cap, and low-cap cryptocurrencies.

For example, it's common to see portfolios with a 50-30-20 split between large, mid, and low-cap cryptocurrencies, respectively. This spread can let you see significant short-term and long-term growth without too much risk.

Many analysts recommend that more than 50% of a portfolio be Bitcoin, while some investors choose to invest in Bitcoin only. These investors are referred to as Bitcoin maximalists — they believe all other cryptocurrencies will eventually go to zero, as they believe Bitcoin will innovate and do what competing altcoins are trying to do. As said before, this depends on your risk tolerance and portfolio style. We take a bullish approach and believe the market is big enough to have more than one cryptocurrency.

Markowitz optimization models

The Markowitz optimization model is a fundamental part of portfolio construction for traditional asset managers. This model birthed the Modern Portfolio Theory, which started the quantitative investing revolution. Nowadays, many quantitative models optimize your portfolio allocation, but it is essential to acknowledge that these models are built on somewhat unrealistic assumptions and can yield unwanted results.

For instance, the Markowitz optimization model assumes that the expected returns of your assets are known and deterministic, and that their returns follow a normal distribution. In plain English, Markowitz believes returns are not random.

This could produce extreme outlier conclusions; for instance, you could have ten assets in your portfolio, and this model will tell you to only invest in 2 or 3, leaving you with an illusion of diversification.

While quantitative models reduce human biases and errors in investing, it is dangerous to use them as a black box and blindly follow their recommendations. Most of these models use historical data and assume the future will be similar to the past. It is therefore vital to use these models only as recommendations, especially in the crypto markets.

Quantitative portfolio allocation

There are many quantitative allocation strategies you can use to determine your portfolio's weighting scheme. Here are some common allocation weight strategies.

- **Market cap weighted:** This strategy allocates according to the size of the token's market cap. More capital is allocated to the largest tokens by market cap, which is common for indexes.

- **Equal weighted:** This strategy allocates equally across tokens. This increases diversification and gives more exposure to tokens with a small or medium market cap.

- **Fundamental weighted:** This strategy allocates based on fundamental characteristics like usage of the cryptocurrency. This is "value"-based, but accounting figures could be accompanied by or introduce random results that obscure the real signal.

- **Risk-weighted:** This strategy allocates higher weights to tokens with low risk, and lower weight to the token with increased risk. This is intuitive but can fail during market trend reversals, as low-risk assets typically deliver lower returns.

- **Equal risk contribution weighted:** This strategy allocates based on each token's risk contribution to the final portfolio. So each token will have the same contribution to overall risk.

- **Max Sharpe ratio weighted:** The Sharpe ratio is a measure of the risk-adjusted return of a portfolio. In other words, it measures whether an investment's returns are worth the risk. This strategy allocates to assets that provide the optimal Sharpe ratio of the final portfolio. This maximizes the risk-adjusted returns.

- **Mean-variance weighted:** This strategy allocates based on the best risk and returns trade-offs. This is related to Markowitz optimization. It allows investors to choose weights that offer the highest expected return for a target variance or the lowest variance for a target expected return. Variance measures how far a set of numbers are spread out from their average expected value.

- **Black-Litterman weighted:** This strategy allocates based on best risk-return trade-offs and investor views. This lets the investors incorporate their absolute or relative ideas on the future performance of tokens into their weighting scheme. Think of this as a hybrid of mean-variance with an investor's subjective views.

Computing quantitative portfolio weights is no easy task. That's why we developed Token Metrics. Our platform automates this for crypto investors so they don't have to bother with technical details.

Rebalancing your portfolio

Since prices will fluctuate over time, this will cause your initial portfolio weights to change. Other factors to consider are your ever-changing financial situation, your future needs, and your risk tolerance. If any of these things change, you will need to readjust your portfolio accordingly. After comparing the new weight with the old one, investors are supposed to determine which ones are overweight or underweight. "Overweight" means you have a lot more of an asset than your allocation strategy recommends, and "underweight" means you have a lot less.

Typically traders and investors select a time-horizon for a periodic rebalancing of their portfolio. This varies between daily, weekly, monthly, quarterly, and annually. Regardless of your trading or investment strategy, the key is to stick to whatever rebalancing period you select. This helps eliminate the emotions of trading or investing. Once your rebalancing period approaches, determine which overweight assets you need to reduce and by how much, then sell off the excess assets to get back to your desired allocation weight. Then take the proceeds from selling off the excess weights and buy more of the underweight assets.

The beauty of periodic rebalancing is that it literally forces you to buy low and sell high. This is the secret to making money as an investor. Buying low and selling high is more challenging than it seems. Buying low means buying when the market is going down and at times crashing.

This is when you get the best discounts, as assets are underpriced. Selling high means selling when the market is going up and people think it will never end.

Most investors lose money because they only want to buy when assets are going up and don't have the confidence to buy when assets are going down. This means they only buy when assets are overpriced and sell when assets are underpriced, decreasing the chances of making money. The trick in investing is to buy from pessimists and sell to optimists.

You want to buy from people who think an asset is dead and never coming back, then sell it to people who feel an asset is going to the moon and beyond. If you master this, you are well on your way to becoming a great investor. Periodic portfolio rebalancing based on weights helps you automate this.

It is necessary to note that when rebalancing and re-adjusting your portfolio, you should take a moment to consider the tax implications of selling assets at a particular time. One of your rebalancing strategy's critical components is understanding your transaction costs and their effects on your profits and losses.

When you rebalance frequently, you need your returns to be greater than rebalancing costs to make a profit. The more frequent the rebalancing, the more transaction costs you pay. There is statistical evidence that the more you rebalance and trade, the less likely you will make a profit — identifying profitable opportunities that outweigh transaction costs can be hard.

The bottom line

Determine your asset allocation strategy. Are you a long-term investor or a short-term trader? Determine a periodic rebalancing time-horizon to reevaluate your portfolio weights, sell your overweight assets, and use the proceeds to buy your underweight assets. This forces you to automate the process of buying low and selling high — the secret to making money as an investor.

CHAPTER 7

Introduction to Fundamental Analysis

CHAPTER 7

Introduction to Fundamental Analysis

What is fundamental analysis?

"Beauty is in the eye of the beholder." It's a common saying among the fundamental analysts of financial markets. Many factors can affect a company's value as a result of various macro and microeconomic forces.

A macroeconomic force is a significant event that affects a regional or national economy, like the economy of a continent or a country. A microeconomic force could be the impact of a decision that a person makes on a market's economy.

For different entities, all these forces will have different impacts. Though fundamental analysis is subjective, there's merit in understanding companies under a broad framework: it lets us compare one company to another.

Methods for evaluating a company depend on many factors. The macroeconomic environment, entry barriers, and management are some of the most critical factors. Token Metrics has tried to borrow these concepts to create a framework for analyzing crypto assets.

We were also mindful of the differences between crypto assets and traditional financial assets while developing the framework.

We've identified over 29 different factors across nine categories for crypto assets. Then we coupled our unique human knowledge with automated machine learning.

These algorithms help us weigh our data points to analyze vast amounts of information and optimize our data points for crypto assets that deliver the best returns. Doing so, we arrive at fundamental scores of various assets using our fundamental ratings.

We use a fluid model because we understand that the crypto industry is fast-paced, so our model needs to change if we want to keep up. We intend to regularly backtest our models, adjust the weights, and even add or remove some factors.

The different categories we look into are initial screening questions, market standing, liquidity, reputation, team, marketing, development, security, scarcity, and quantitative performance metrics.

Initial screening questions

The crypto market has over 6,000 crypto assets — analyzing all of them could take a lifetime. To reduce the amount of time spent on unfavorable projects, it makes sense to have initial screening questions that can be used as a filter.

These questions are meant for pre-market cryptocurrencies, projects that are not yet trading. These are typically tokens sold through private or public token sales, also known as initial coin offerings (ICOs).

With the absence of trading activity, these initial screening questions could save investors money.

Large insider discount

Were tokens sold at a discount greater than 80% in a prior round? This usually is a warning sign, no matter how great a project is. If a project gives discounts to insiders like venture capitalists and other early angel investors, it creates selling pressure when the token gets listed on exchanges.

For instance, if investors privately purchased a token at $0.10, and the project sells the same token to the general public, retail investors, at $1.00, early investors are incentivized to sell part or all of their tokens to lock in an immediate 10X return on their investment.

If there's a project you like with a significant insider discount, it is usually best to wait until insiders have sold and selling pressure has bottomed before looking to accumulate a position. This is where insider vesting is essential.

Insider vesting

Are the team's tokens locked for more than six months after those tokens start trading on exchanges?

Projects that give insiders discounts often add vesting or lockup terms to purchased tokens to prevent insiders from selling them, or as it's often called colloquially, "dumping on retail investors." Vesting is when team members aren't allowed to sell their tokens until a year or two after the initial token sale, and it shows that the team is committed to further developing the project.

Vesting terms can vary. A standard vesting schedule for investors is one to two years, with distributions every month, quarter, or six months.

For instance, a project with one-year vesting, quarterly distribution, and no cliff would give investors 25% of their purchased tokens upon issuance and 25% every three months until investors have received all their purchased tokens.

Insiders are usually large investors like venture capitalists or angel investors. Investors should be aware of vesting schedules for insiders, as their large investments can turn into large sells that move the trading market for a particular cryptocurrency.

It's common for traders or investors to avoid buying tokens on token unlock days for insiders. Suppose the community anticipates a quarterly distribution of tokens to seed round venture capitalists on April 30th. In that case, traders might sell their positions a week before, while investors might wait a month or so for insiders to sell their tokens before buying.

Fully decentralized?

Does the community own more than 50% of the tokens? For a cryptocurrency project to be considered fully decentralized, this should be the case. (Alternatively, the core team should hold less than 50% of the total token supply.)

This is a crucial screening question because if the team holds more than 50% of the token supply, they control the market for their token and community governance. But if the community owns the majority of the token supply, then the market and governance are democratized, which is one of the major philosophies of crypto.

Market standing

Competition

Competition is a critical factor that affects the market standing of cryptos. It measures how innovative the projects are in the market, and where they stand among different projects. Based on the project's technical value and use cases, we will determine who competes with a given crypto.

For example, Ethereum is ranked top among its competitors. In terms of its technical value, it is a layer-2 open source platform for users to create decentralized applications.

Token Metrics will consider those with similar networks or use cases to be its competitors, like EOS. Then we will consider other factors, like liquidity and reputation, to determine their competition in the market. Since Bitcoin is a peer-to-peer payment platform for users, we don't consider it similar to Ethereum.

Use cases

A significant factor for evaluating a cryptocurrency is its use case. People expect cryptocurrencies to meet an unmet need in the market, or to otherwise solve some problem. To adopt crypto is to adopt new technology.

People will not use cryptocurrency if it doesn't save their time or money.

As mentioned earlier, Bitcoin offers a new financial payment method while Ethereum makes contracts on its network more intelligent. Use cases can usually be divided into financial use cases and non-financial use cases. Financial use cases include lending and borrowing, while non-financial use cases include store of value or gaming. Use cases will also vary in different industries like real estate, the Internet of Things, and healthcare.

Again, we will emphasize the importance of researching a particular cryptocurrency — if use cases can't be clearly described, it might be a scam.

Token utility

A token is different from a coin. A token can be the utility that a company provides to a token holder. There are two types: utility tokens and security tokens. Security tokens function as investment contracts that let people trade on exchanges, or treat the tokens as collateral when they need to borrow assets from exchanges.

Utility tokens provide users with the rights to take advantage of the network's capabilities. Common rights of utility tokens include governance and voting. When people hold a governance token, they can vote to change a project's parameters so that it better meets their needs.

Token economic incentives

Economic incentives are a powerful tool for decentralized solutions, letting economy participants be trusted to work towards a clear goal instead of being manual supervised. Economic incentives motivate stakeholders to act in the community's best interest, like decentralizing the network.

Liquidity

Liquidity is the ease at which an underlying asset can be converted into a major form of money, like the US dollar. At the same time, the price of that underlying asset should not be affected. It is therefore vital to ensure that a liquid market allows the buying and selling of the asset at stable and transparent prices.

Token Metrics uses data from exchanges to measure their liquidity, checking certain stats like 24-hour trading volume, market capitalization, and the number of buy and sell orders.

Fiat-to-crypto trading pairs

Fiat on-ramps are services that exchange your fiat currency for crypto. Fiat on-ramps for tokens imply that these tokens do not have to rely on other tokens for liquidity.

Percentage of total supply circulating

Token supply releases often happen in tranches. Tokens that are traded in the public market account for circulating supply, while the total supply is the maximum amount of tokens issued. If more tokens are available, it can put downward pressure on the price. As circulating supply can be used to calculate a token's market capitalization, the more the percentage of circulating supply, the larger the market capitalization we get.

Liquidity ratio (trading volume to market cap)

In financial markets, and especially in mutual funds, the liquidity ratio measures the proportion of daily trading volume to an asset's total market cap. The liquidity ratio helps in understanding how liquid a market is. Liquidity can have a smoothing on a market, whereas illiquid markets are often volatile.

An excellent turn-over ratio is usually between 10% and 50%. Anything lower than 10% and the market is not liquid enough. Anything over 50% and the market mainly consists of short-term traders and speculators, with few long-term believers in the market. Suppose a cryptocurrency has a total market cap of $5 million but a daily trading volume of $10 million. That would yield a liquidity ratio of 2. This means this cryptocurrency is held by two buyers on average each day. If we were

long-term value investors, we would avoid this cryptocurrency now —
these numbers mean day traders mainly hold it, or there is artificial market manipulation happening in this market. Neither is a good sign.

Listed exchanges

A cryptocurrency exchange is where people can buy and sell their tokens
for other currencies or traditional currencies, like the US dollar or euro.
These types of exchanges usually include trading platforms, direct trading, and brokers.

Trading platforms charge a fee for each transaction and connect buyers.
Direct trading provides a place for peer-to-peer trading, such as decentralized exchanges. Brokers set a price for buyers on these exchanges.

Investors will consider several factors before they decide to trade on an exchange. The factors include the reputation of the exchanges, exchange
ratio, trading fees, and payment methods.

Popular exchanges will provide high liquidity for traders, and at the
same time, the turnover ratio of their assets will be high. Exchanges like
Coinbase, Binance, Bittrex, and Kraken are currently very popular.

Reputation

Early reputable investors

The reputation of early investors can show the strength of a project. Reputable investors only invest in projects they believe in, and they of course
expect a good return on their investment. These investors could also be
crucial in developing the project to obtain partnerships that drive growth.
Investors like Andreessen Horowitz, Coinbase Ventures, and Blockchain
Capital are some of the reputable investors in the crypto market.

Litigations against the teams

If the company or a key member was involved in a scandal, this could hurt the project's long-term potential. Alleged (or actual) unethical behavior causes terrible press for the project. Users are less likely to want to be involved with a project that's been outed for its unethical practices.

Public team

How public-facing is the team? Many companies offer Ask Me Anything (AMA) sessions to put themselves out there and clarify their project. This lets companies gain more exposure for their projects, as well as potentially gain more users and partners.

Anonymous teams are prevalent in crypto. Just consider the unknown Bitcoin founder, Satoshi Nakamoto. But a lot of crypto scams have been executed by anonymous teams as well. That's why we believe teams that keep a public profile are safer, as there is someone to hold publicly accountable.

Team

Number of team members

We often observe Github projects having just one or two developers, but we are looking for the team to have more than ten members. We are not saying that a team with fewer members cannot perform well on their projects, but we prefer those with more than ten team members for sake of a reasonable work allocation. Not all team members have the same background, but we prefer those with diversified backgrounds in software engineering and finance.

Number of all-star team members

We consider a person with more than two years of experience in a publicly-traded company or a top twenty-five market cap blockchain project to be an all-star team member. This type of person usually has a background in software engineering, architecture, consulting, or investment banking. To see how a project could go, we focus on the project's management team and pay attention to how many talented people are on the team. A team with five all-star members is a strong team.

Marketing

Number of community members

The number of community members can represent a project's popularity. A project's community size should be evaluated with the average cryptocurrency community size. In large communities, the leadership teams answer questions from users interested in their projects. The leadership also updates their news of token sales or airdrops to the community. These communities are typically found on Telegram, Twitter, Discord, and Reddit, linked from a company's website.

Monthly website traffic

Website visits are an excellent proxy to gauge a project's mindshare. Before investing in a project, people visit the website to understand more about it. Site visits are a way to determine customer awareness. This data shows how well the team advertises and promotes what they are doing.

Company website and whitepaper

The company website serves as the primary source of information for any project. Any attempt to hide information is a red flag. Details like the roadmap, team members, and privacy policies should be readily available there. To assess a coin, we have to dive into its technical specifications. Cryptocurrency whitepapers outline these details for a project — these documents describe everything about how it works, which can massively influence an investment decision. Don't forget to read whitepapers before investing!

Development

Years in business before token issuance

The date when a company is founded and the date when it launches a cryptocurrency tell us how long a company has been in business before requesting money from investors. Companies that have been in business for a while before issuing their tokens are typically less risky. Some projects launch a few months after the companies are founded without any product, which can suggest a scam or money grab based on just a white paper. Teams that have been building and operating for a long time before raising money usually perform better.

Availability of competent developers and leaders

Users tend to trust a team with well-known members in the industry. This type of person in the team can usually drive the development progress and articulate the project's vision and strategy. Having experienced developers and leaders in the team could be an essential driver for the project.

Security

Security is arguably the most critical function of a blockchain used for value transfer. Blockchains often claim to be decentralized, and therefore security becomes crucial as that decentralization leaves no one liable for losses. Crypto hacks are common, and if there are security flaws in the blockchain, then a hacker will almost inevitably find them.

Consensus mechanism

Consensus is the heart of a blockchain. Consensus mechanisms exist to mitigate so-called "double-spend" attacks, in which a user makes a new transaction with the same data already validated by the network. They are fault-tolerant systems for reaching specific agreements within groups, especially in decentralized systems. Fault tolerance is the property that enables a system to continue operating correctly in the event of failure.

Proof of Work (PoW) is one of the most common consensus mechanisms — it's what Bitcoin uses. PoW requires a participant node to prove that the work has been done and submitted so that the users are qualified to add a new transaction to the blockchain. Proof of Stake (PoS) is another consensus algorithm that comes with low costs and low energy requirements. It is less risky for miners to attack the network since their mining power is based on the proportion of the coins they hold.

The way a blockchain arrives at its consensus determines the security of the blockchain. It's essential to understand how a blockchain achieves its consensus.

Governance

Most companies and organizations in the real world are centralized, which means there is usually a leadership team governing them. But since blockchains are decentralized, they need a unique form of governance to meet the needs of users and developers alike.

Four communities are typically involved in blockchain governance: core developers, node operators, token holders, and the blockchain team. The governance structure is built to protect community interests.

Blockchain governance can be categorized into two types: off-chain governance and on-chain governance. Off-chain governance is used to promote balance between different communities, and it is relatively centralized. On-chain governance is achieved with built-in voting mechanisms, and it optimizes the requirements and needs of the network.

The "Blockchain Trilema"

During the ICO mania in 2017, various projects promised the moon to investors and did not deliver. Ethereum co-founder Vitalik Buterin believes in the Blockchain Trilemma, which states that blockchains cannot achieve security, decentralization, and scalability simultaneously — they must sacrifice at least one of these traits. For example, a blockchain can have security and decentralization, but cannot achieve scalability.

Solving the Blockchain Trilemma is the holy grail for blockchain developers. Projects that currently claim to be blockchains and promise better security, decentralization, and scalability than Bitcoin or Ethereum have yet to deliver on these promises.

Scarcity

Token burn

A token burn is a mechanism for creating scarcity in a token supply. Burning is an indirect way to redistribute profits or cash flows to token holders. The scarcity puts upward pressure on the token's price.

Nature of the supply

Whether inflationary or deflationary, token supply matters. As it is related to monetary policy, we will see how the value of a token changes in relation to the supply amount. The nature of a token supply can be a measurement to see the scarcity of crypto, and we consider those with deflationary supply to be scarce crypto.

A deflationary supply means that the company has already fixed the total amount of token supply — a billion tokens, for example. If the company does not initially set a fixed supply, it is considered either inflationary or reducing inflationary. We consider these types of supply to be less scarce. The EOS blockchain offers an example of an inflationary token supply with a fixed 4.5% inflation rate. At the same time, Ethereum is an example of a reducing inflationary token supply, with the annual inflation rate decreasing and approaching zero, in an asymptotic line.

Stock-To-Flow model

The concept of Stock-to-Flow was published for the first time in March 2019, creating a value model for Bitcoin. Bitcoin is considered to be a scarce digital object like gold and silver. In the article, the author quantified the scarcity of Bitcoin by using the Stock-to-Flow model.

Perception of gold and silver scarcity is heightened because the price changes in these assets will be insignificant even if the supplies double. Therefore, scarcity here refers to those assets with a lower price elasticity of supply.

Equation 7.1 shows the formula that quantifies scarcity:

$$SF = Stock/Flow$$

"Stock" represents the size of existing reserves of assets, while "Flow" is the yearly production of the asset. The inverse of the Stock-to-Flow model measures the annual supply growth rate. Equation 7.2 shows the formula for annual supply growth rate:

$$Annual\ Supply\ Growth\ Rate = Flow/Stock$$

"Stock" represents the size of existing reserves of assets, while "Flow" is the yearly production of the asset.

Thus Equation 7.3 becomes:

$$Stock\text{-}to\text{-}Flow = 1\ /\ Annual\ Supply\ Growth\ Rate$$

Stock-to-Flow provides a simple quantitative framework for analyzing price trends in Bitcoin. It's an indicator with robust explanatory power that makes Bitcoin comparable to gold and its relatives.

Table 7.1 shows a comparison between different commodities.

	Stock (tn)	Flow (tn)	SF	Supply Growth	Price $/Oz	Market Value
Gold	185,000	3,000	62	1.6% $	1300 $	8,417,500,000,000 $
Silver	550,000	25,000	22	4.5% $	16 $	308,000,000,000 $
Palladium	244	215	1.1	88.1% $	1400 $	11,956,000,000 $
Platinum	86	229	0.4	266.7% $	800 $	2,400,000,000 $

Table 7.1: Comparison between commodities

The Stock-to-Flow of gold is 62, while silver has the second-highest at 22. Back in 2019, Bitcoin had 17.5 million coins, and the supply was 700,000/year. Using the formula, we can determine a Stock-to-Flow of Bitcoin at 25, right between the Stock-to-Flow of gold and silver.

Bitcoin Difficulty Ribbon

The Bitcoin Difficulty Ribbon is the Bitcoin network's mining difficulty band index. It was first proposed by Vinny Lingham, founder of the Civic project.

So what is the "difficulty" of a cryptocurrency? It's the value that measures how hard it is to find a hash that will be lower than the target defined by the system. The hash rate is used to measure the processing power of the Bitcoin network. Bitcoin's effective hash rate is calculated daily, based on the actual number of blocks found by miners each day.

The difficulty of Bitcoin changes every 2,016 blocks, and the target is a 256-digit number.

Equation 7.4 shows how to calculate the difficulty of Bitcoin:

$$Difficulty = Difficulty\ Target\ /\ Current\ Target$$

The difficulty band consists of a simple moving average of the Bitcoin network difficulty, showing the impact of the miner's throw on Bitcoin price action.

As new coins are mined, miners generally sell a portion of the tokens to cover production costs, which creates downward price pressure. The least potent miners have to sell more tokens to keep the machines running because they use more electricity for each token received.

When all the tokens sold are still not enough to cover the cost of mining, most miners are already in the shutdown process, and the hashing capacity and network difficulty are reduced — the difficulty band shrinks.

When the climb slope of the entire network difficulty band decreases and overlaps, only strong miners can continue mining. These powerful miners would need to sell a smaller percentage of Bitcoin to maintain operations, which would reduce the market Bitcoin sell-off and provide more room for price increases.

The area where the mining difficulty band contracts or overlaps would be the best time to build a Bitcoin position. For example, when the vast majority of miners are already down and the time is entering the end of the bear market period, the coin price could bottom out and rebound.

Quantitative performance metrics

Sharpe ratio

When people make investments, they usually care about the risk and return of an asset. The Sharpe ratio is one of the most commonly used portfolio management metrics when measuring assets. It's also called "risk-adjusted returns," since it provides us with the relationship between return on investment and risks.

Equation 7.5 shows the Sharpe Ratio formula:

Sharpe Ratio = (Return of Asset or Portfolio - Risk Free Rate) / (Standard Deviation of Asset or PortfolioExcess Returns)

Based on this formula, we consider the assets with a high ratio to perform well in the market. If the Sharpe Ratio of a coin is over three, we generally consider it to be in a healthy condition, while a coin below one is performing poorly.

Network value to transactions ratio (NVT ratio)

The NVT ratio is also called the price-to-earnings (P/E) ratio in the crypto market. To understand their relationship, we will start with the P/E ratio in the stock market.

Traditional financial markets use the P/E ratio to assess a company's stock performance. Investors can estimate whether the stock prices of a company are overvalued or undervalued.

This ratio presents the price an investor is willing to pay for the stock's earnings per dollar. If the P/E ratio of a stock is high, it means the investor is willing to pay a high price for getting one dollar of this stock.

In any case, this doesn't mean investors always welcome a stock with a high P/E ratio, since P/E can be thrown off during a volatile market.

Equation 7.6 shows the formula for calculating a P/E ratio:

P/E = Stock Price/Earnings Per Share

Now let's bring this to the crypto market. Willy Woo introduced the concept of NVT ratio, where the money flowing through the network (transaction money) is used as a proxy metric for reflecting the value of the network.

Equation 7.7 shows the NVT formula. As you can see, we use the daily transaction value instead of earnings per share and network value instead of stock price to calculate NVT.

NVT = Network Value/Daily Transaction Amount

High NVT ratios can indicate high speculative value. We saw NVTs above 100 in the early days of Bitcoin, indicating an increased investment win rate.

By using the NVT Ratio, investors could predict the potential of a bubble in the crypto market. But predicting a bubble before it happens is tricky — a price spike doesn't necessarily mean that the assets are in a bubble. People usually consider Bitcoin to be in bubble territory if the NVT ratio is over 95.

Market-value-to-realized-value (MVRV) ratio

In 2018, Nic Carter of Castle Island Ventures worked with Antoine Le Calvez of Blockchain.info to develop the MVRV metric. Equation 7.8 shows the calculation for MVRV:

MVRV Ratio = Market Value/Realized Value

Market value is also known as market capitalization. By calculating market value, you can multiply the trading prices of a coin on exchanges by the number of coins mined.

Realized Value helps eliminate the coins that are unused or lost from the total market capitalization. Here we introduce a new concept: unspent transaction output, or UTXO. This is the amount of digital currency remaining after a transaction is executed. Instead of using the number of mined coins on exchanges, we use UTXOs as a factor to calculate the realized value.

Another factor is the price of UTXOs. The trading prices we use in market capitalization are replaced by the prices when UTXOs last moved. Then, we simply multiply these two factors to get the realized value of the coin.

We introduce the MVRV ratio because we can use the framework to view the market from two perspectives, which would support us to analyze the market critically.

Here, we provide a framework of market dichotomy:

- Speculators vs. HODLers.

- High time preference vs. low time preference.

- Irrational exuberance vs. uncertainty acclimation.

When the market value goes below a 1:1 ratio to the realized value, we would consider the coin to be undervalued.

On June 26, 2019, Bitcoin's MVRV reached 2.57 (Figure 7.1) and then entered a decline channel until December 17, 2019, when the MVRV dropped to 1.18 before beginning a slow recovery.

Bitcoin MVRV Ratio

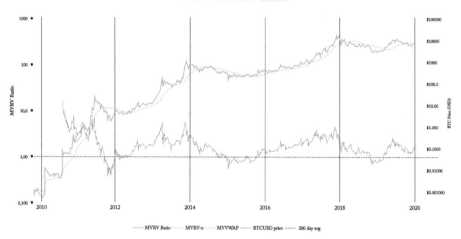

Figure 7.1: Bitcoin MVRV Ratio

Bitcoin with an MVRV value below 1.5 generally implies a lower valuation, and a value above 3.5 indicates a higher valuation. Historically, there have been three times when Bitcoin's MVRV value has been below 1, which implies a historical bottom: late 2011, early 2015, and early 2019. After each of these three historical lows, Bitcoin entered an upward cycle.

Mayer Multiplier

Created by renowned investor and podcast host Trace Mayer, the Mayer Multiplier is defined as a multiple of the current Bitcoin price on a 200-day moving average. The equivalent gives a ratio relative to time and past transaction prices.

Equation 7.9 shows the Mayer Multiplier:

Mayer Multiplier = Bitcoin Market Price/200-Day Market Value

When using Mayer Multipliers, there are two critical values: 1 and 2.4.

The significance of a multiplier of 1 is simple: any value above 1 means that Bitcoin's prices have risen to a 200-day low, and any value below 1 means that prices have fallen to a minimum.

Secondly, any multiplier above the 2.4 threshold historically indicates the beginning of a speculative bubble. Consider December 2017, when Bitcoin reached a new high and the Mayer multiple (Figure 7.2) reached an abnormally high 3.65. Later in June 2019, when Bitcoin reached another new high, the Mayer multiple also reached 2.48. Using simulations based on historical data, Mayer inferred that the best long-term investment returns could be obtained by hoarding Bitcoin when the Mayer multiple is below 2.4.

Bitcoin Mayer Multiple

Figure 7.2: Bitcoin Mayer Multiple.

The bottom line

Fundamental analysis helps you make better investment decisions. Fortunately, Token Metrics provides our customers with a reasonable fundamental analysis that stands the test of the market in the long term. By combining the fundamental analysis with technical analysis, we believe Token Metrics can help you make your critical investment decisions wisely.

CHAPTER 8

Introduction to Trading

CHAPTER 8

Introduction to Trading

What is trading?

Trading is the art and science of buying low and selling high. Day traders are concerned with short-term price movements while other traders might hold positions for days, weeks, weeks, or months. Figure 8.1 shows Bitcoin's 2017 price increase from $6,000 to $20,000 in just two months — it's enough to entice anyone to start trading.

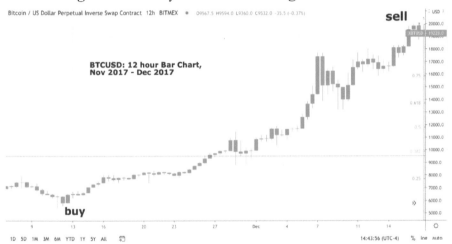

Figure 8.1: Bitcoin price in 2017

Margin trading

Margin trading lets a trader use leverage to increase their position size with borrowed money. If a trader has a thousand dollars, they can borrow another thousand and increase the amount of money they make, assuming their investment choices pay out.

Many crypto exchanges offer customers the chance to use leverage in a massive way. This offer can be a trap, as novice traders find out quickly that the more they are levered, the quicker they can be forced to liquidate a trade if it goes against them.

The best time to use margin is when a trade is already going your way, and you wish to strengthen the amount of profit you will gain if a more substantial, lengthier trend should be detected.

This can be an advantageous way to make money in crypto if you've learned how to play the margin game.

Options trading

An option gives the holder the right (but not the obligation) to buy or sell an underlying instrument or futures contract. The former is called a "call," the latter is called a "put." Calls let you bet that an asset is going up. A put option lets you profit if an asset declines.

Options trading can have advantages for new traders — if you deal in calls, for example, your losses are limited to the premium that you paid. For example, if you pay $0.50 for a call option, and the market crashes, all you lose is that $0.50 share in the contract.

A key trait of options is that they have an expiration date. You only have a certain amount of time to be right about your position. Options also tend to decline in value as time goes on — this is called "time decay." So if you buy an option and the market in question just sits still, the options will lose a little value each day. This may be less of a problem in crypto, as moves of 5% or more are commonplace.

Traders frequently use options to go outside their usual short-term strategy and bet on a more extended trend. Institutional traders use this strategy a lot because the risk is well-defined and the upside can be quite significant when they are right.

If the data is available, it can illuminate the overall "put-call ratio" for a market, letting you see how market participants are positioned. For example, when put-call ratios show that participants own enormous amounts of one type of option, it can be a contrarian indicator to make a bet in the opposite direction of the herd.

Futures trading

Futures trading offers an opportunity to trade an instrument without actually owning the instrument itself. Futures contracts require a deposit in an account, letting traders put down a portion of the contract's value as collateral of sorts.

The bigger the contract's notional value, the more money you have to put down to trade it. So futures exchanges of what they call "mini contracts" make it easier for retail traders to get involved.

Order types

Choosing the correct order type is an essential part of profitable trading.

Market order

A market order instructs your broker or exchange to buy at the current market price. You have to be very careful about using market orders in crypto.

If you decide to buy after a market has started rallying, or decide to sell when it is declining, then the price where your order gets filled may be very different from the price you saw on your screen.

Market orders have their uses because the crypto market moves quickly. That said, avoiding the market can be a way to create discipline and avoid the fear of missing out (FOMO) on a big move once it starts. New traders frequently fall into the trap of "FOMO-ing" into positions only to buy at the top and sell at the bottom of a downward move.

Limit order

A limit order specifies the price that you are willing to pay to get into a trade. A buy limit order is usually placed below the current market price, letting you take advantage of a dip. A sell limit order is generally placed above the current market price and represents the lowest price a trader is willing to accept for their assets. Limit orders can add a level of discipline to trading, particularly when combined with technical analysis strategy.

But they do have a downside: if the market in question never reaches the price you are willing to buy or sell, your order will never be filled. So the execution of the market order requires good analysis, tactics, and patience.

Stop order

A stop order is most frequently used to limit a position's loss. A stop order is placed below the market in an extended position to limit a loss if the trader is wrong about the market going up. Once a stop order is triggered, it becomes a market order.

When you see extreme prices, it is frequently because many traders all had their stops placed at the same level. Learning where to put a stop order is necessary for successful trading. Stop orders can also be used to enter a position. If a trader thinks a big move will start if a market rises above or falls below a certain point, a stop order can trigger an automatic market order once a certain level is breached.

Stop-limit order

As you might guess, a stop-limit order combines a stop and a limit order. This type of order specifies both a stop price where the order is activated, and a limit price.

Once this stop is triggered, the trader defines a maximum or minimum price at which the trade will be executed. Since crypto is a very fast-moving market, there may not be liquidity at your specified price.

If that is the case, even if the market trades through your order and it should be executed, it may not get filled.

How to use order types

The essential order type to use in crypto is a stop-loss order. Generally speaking, you don't want to risk any more than 1% to 2% of your overall capital. That way, if you are wrong on several short-term trades, you still have the money to continue.

The best use of market orders is to take profits on a long or short position when a coin is either pumping rapidly (long) or dumping (short). When you have a massive winning trade, it sometimes can be challenging to come up with a price for a limit order when you'd rather ring the cash register and pat yourself on the back. Limit orders have a variety of uses.

If you want a coin only at a specific price, then a limit order would be appropriate. Stop limit orders are helpful if you suspect that you are not the only one with a stop at the level in question. In a long position, you might want to define the limit where your order is executed.

This could prevent you from a price manipulation where the price dislocates 5% below your stop order price, only to come roaring back. Stop-limit orders can prevent you from getting hosed.

Regular limits can help if you don't have time to sit and watch the market all day. If you have to walk away, you might also want to set a level for taking profits if you are not in front of the screen. Regular limit orders are also useful for self-discipline. If you have a winning trade, you might be tempted to think the market is going to the moon (long) or to zero (short). Having a limit in the market creates automatic discipline for booking your profits.

There's an old saying from the legacy markets of Wall Street: "You can never get fired for taking profits."

Finally, looking at order books on exchanges can help see what big traders are doing. Figure 8.2 highlights a big buy order just below market price.

	Orderbook		Grouping None ▼
	41,419		
Bid Size (BTC)	Bid Price (USDT)	Ask Price (USDT)	Ask Size (BTC)
0.2500	41,415	41,426	0.0500
0.0002	41,412	41,427	3.7669
0.4600	41,411	41,428	0.1856
0.5083	41,410	41,430	0.0072
0.9335	41,409	41,433	0.0050
0.1962	41,407	41,434	5.7875
0.8012	41,405	41,437	0.0533
0.0532	41,403	41,439	0.2373
0.1086	41,401	41,440	10.0624
7.2849	41,400	41,443	0.9305

Figure 8.2: Buy Order

Technical analysis

Technical analysis, often shortened to TA, is the study of market price action. It's essentially the art and science of figuring out market periods. Markets go through quiet and active periods — they can trend or trade in a range. One of the best examples of a range trade is Figure 8.3, the weekly chart of Ethereum showing close to two years of sideways action.

Types of technical analysis

We break TA down into the "quantitative" and the "qualitative."

Quantitative TA

Quantitative TA uses algorithms or artificial intelligence to sense patterns and generate signals for traders. The most common type of quantitative TA is a moving average crossover model.

You could program a charting computer to turn bullish if certain moving averages crossed above or below another moving average in the old days. We'll cover moving averages in depth later.

With quantitative TA, the algorithm generates signals for humans to make their buy and sell decisions. Token Metrics brings this form of TA to the retail investor at an affordable cost using its price prediction tool, which plots out a future path based on complex mathematical modeling.

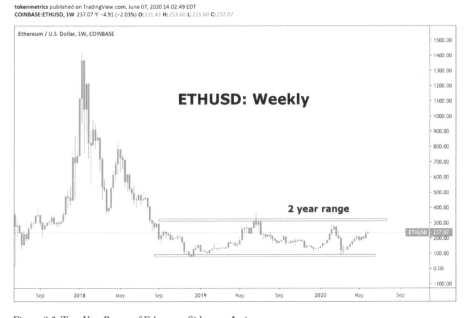

Figure 8.3: Two-Year Range of Ethereum Sideways Action.

In some quantitative systems, the AI will execute the trade itself. TA at this level of sophistication is normal at the institutional level.

Qualitative TA

Qualitative TA comes in many different types, which may seem overwhelming at first. Some bloviate on Twitter and throw an occasional chart at the low end, trying to convince people that their idea is a good idea. Crypto Twitter has its place as a source of possible charts.

Qualitative technical analysis is an art. We liken it to playing a musical instrument. You have to get a tool that works for you, and then you have to practice. The most common charting program of choice in crypto is TradingView, which has a wide variety of chart types and indicators. With qualitative technical analysis, you can pick which charts and indicators work for you.

Trend trading

Capturing profits from a big trend is a process. In crypto, reversals to the upside are usually preceded by a base followed by a high-volume burst. That burst is generally followed by a quiet period.

In 2019, Bitcoin saw one of the best models for a transition from the bottom to an uptrend. In that case, a model, Figure 8.5, the work of technical analyst Richard Wyckoff, helped identify a pattern that allowed for tracking and trading the bottoming process in Bitcoin.

Figure 8.4: Token Metrics Price Prediction Tool

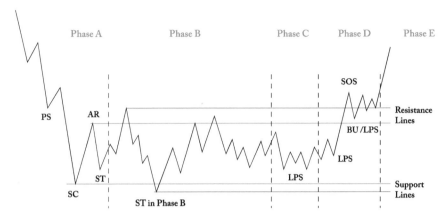

Figure 8.5: Wyckoff Events and Phases

Figure 8.6 shows the trend that unfolded back in 2019, in which Bitcoin moved from $4,000 to $13,000.

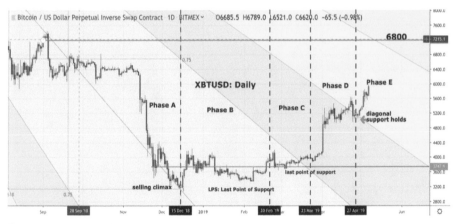

Figure 8.6: Bitcoin trend in 2019

You have to manage your emotions during quiet periods. There can be a lot of noise that discourages you from entering or keeping a long position. This is where you want to rely on TA and the indicators you follow.

If you can establish an initial position, the trend begins and you start generating profit. This creates an opportunity to add to the size of the position, or add leverage. A famous trader once said, "You have to earn the right to take risk." This saying emphasizes a key position: you only want to take a bigger position when you can use profits from the initial trade as a cushion. As the trend develops, the market will test people. People who FOMO in after a strong up move will frequently wind up getting stopped on lower price moves. Even if the coin is in an uptrend, dips will still feel scary. You will have to rely on internal fortitude, your conviction in your idea, and your TA. Once a trend develops, you will want to have a checklist that you watch regularly.

Trading checklist

1. What is the short-term trend over 1-3 days? It can be useful to use a 60-minute, 89-minute, or 12-hour bar chart to look at short-term movement. We discovered the odd time frame of 89 minutes, shown in Figure 8.7, thanks to a famous Wall Street analyst from the 1980s and 1990s.

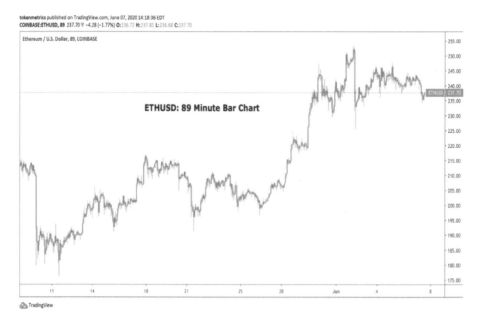

Figure 8.7: Ethereum 89-Minute Bar Chart

2. What are the weekly and monthly trends? For example, you could be catching a big move in an overall bear market, so it's essential to know where you are in the scheme of things (Figure 8.8).

3. Does the market need to consolidate and build steam after a big pump? Remember, nothing goes straight up or straight down.

4. Where would I add to positions?

5. What can I do today to manage my emotions? (Consider working out, meditation, surfing, bike riding, and so on — find your groove in this area.)

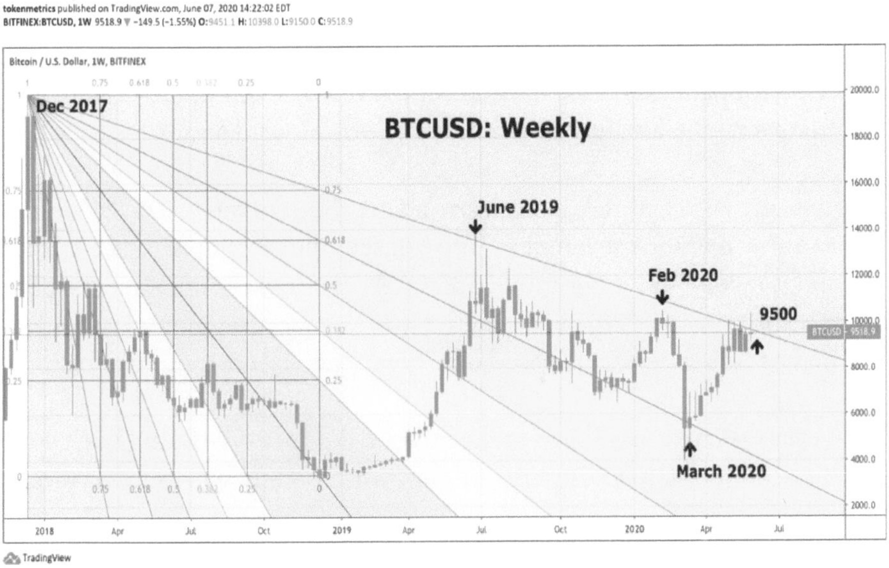

Figure 8.8: 2017 Bitcoin Chart.

One other key aspect of trend trading is to define the type of consolidation phase. Some consolidation phases are quiet, some have broad 20-30% ranges. You don't want big swings in consolidation to take away your ability to see and take advantage of the big trend.

The final question for trend traders is when to get out. If you are long, the best time to get out is when the mass media is writing grandiose articles about the trend's nature.

In a bear crypto market, fear, uncertainty, and doubt (FUD) are high. There can be talk of Bitcoin going to zero. This can be an excellent time to look at crypto Twitter — in 2019, when crypto bears were taking their victory lap, it was time to cover shorts.

How do you use TA?

The best use of TA is for navigation. Just as ancient navigators used the sun, the moon, and the stars to get to their destination, you can use TA to figure out where the market currently is, and where it might go in the future. The first step in navigation is to figure out where the market is relative to the last big move up or down. When looking at a chart, you might want to ask yourself where the previous big up move started, and where it stopped. The same is valid on the downside. Where is the market relative to the last few down moves, both big and small?

Another great use of TA is to learn about the market you're watching. TA can put market movements into context. For example, news comes out about a coin and a big move occurs. At the most simplistic level, the chart helps you see that move relative to recent price action. It also lets you make trading decisions based on where that big move starts and stops.

In summation, you use TA to make informed decisions. Going with your gut can lead to FOMO-ing into trades, which rarely works in crypto.

No matter how experienced or inexperienced you are, TA lets you keep learning. If you are not using TA, you may just be gambling and leaving your profits and losses to chance.

Advanced TA

The science of advanced TA can best be described as using more than one indicator at a time. The art of advanced TA is knowing which indicators to combine and when.

Advanced TA in crypto takes on a unique twist. You first want to look above the market to see where previous down moves started. This is called resistance. Then look below the market and see where any previous bottoms were. This is called support. That might sound basic, but TA becomes advanced when you start mixing indicators. The most advanced work leverages the horizontal perspective offered by support and resistance, combining it with diagonal points. Diagonal points come from some trading indicators made famous by technicians and mathematics from the past. William Gann, Fibonacci, and Ralph Elliot are three people who put together a wide range of indicators to look at a market using diagonal resistance points.

To keep it brief, the diagonal indicators (Figure 8.9) require you to pick relevant highs and lows. TradingView will create sets of diagonal lines, and from there, you can see if any lines appear relevant now or in the past. Then you can make decisions about whether those lines match up with any other analysis or indicators. If not, you can scrap your original drawing and start again.

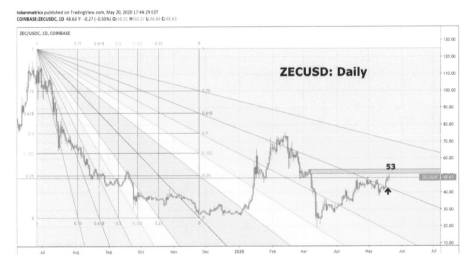

Figure 8.9: Diagonal indicators

In advanced TA, it's easy to get confused. Don't force things, and don't be in a rush. If you don't know "what to do," then don't do anything when it comes to advanced indicators. Keep things as simple as possible!

Advanced TA also involves the use of pattern recognition. The most famous pattern in all of TA is the head and shoulders. Head and shoulders top represents three attempts by bulls to advance a market.

The middle move, called "the head," is the largest of the moves.

The final move up is usually accompanied by the highest level of emotion, followed by big disappointment. If the market then breaks a trend line connecting the bottoms of the three up moves, a down move follows. The nickname for the trend line is the "neckline" (Figure 8.10).

Figure 8.10: An Example of a "neckline" Trend Line.

Shorting

Shorting is the science of trying to profit if the price of an instrument falls. In the conventional stock market, you would borrow shares from somebody who holds them long term, then sell those borrowed shares on the market. When and if the market drops, after that you buy back the shares at the lower price. You return the shares to the owner and keep any money you made in the process.

If you short an instrument and are forced to repurchase it at a higher price, you will lose money. Crypto shorting is typically done with derivative instruments. Derivatives move in parallel with a crypto asset like Bitcoin.

The difference is that while using these derivatives, you don't actually hold the crypto in question. You just use the derivative (usually called a futures contract) to push the buy button for betting up and the sell button for betting down. You decide how much to bet based on what you are willing to risk.

Shorting can be a fantastic way to make money in crypto. When crypto goes down, it can really fall hard, sometimes in 10% increments. On the other hand, when too many people believe a market is going down (shorting), the price rises can be dramatic as short-sellers run to cover their bearish bets.

Shorting can help you make money, but it's even better to understand the mentality of chronic short-sellers (who might even be crypto haters). Some of the biggest rallies in crypto unfold when there are too many short sellers active in the market.

Why most traders lose money

Professional traders work hard and study a lot. Many of the rest lose money because they can't or won't put in the time to go through all the development stages, creating indicators and systems that work.

Perhaps the biggest reason why traders lose money is a lack of discipline. You should only risk 1% or 2% of your account on any single trade. Traders often don't define a stop-loss level ahead of making a trade.

Another reason traders lose money is that they trade too often. So-called "overtrading" can be driven by frustration. But if you have three losing trades in a row, just take a step back and breathe.

Traders also lose money out of boredom. They are so anxious to turn a profit that they make impulsive decisions instead of using TA to help them make decisions. There's an old saying that applies here: "If you don't know what to do, don't do anything." Don't blame the market if you lose money. It is not out to get you. Most traders lose money because it takes training to manage their emotions. Successful professional traders often don't have vivid personalities. Many are quiet, boring people.

The biggest reason traders lose money is that they compete against computer algorithms to think and learn faster than they can. Our advice is to get your hands on any quant-based tool, such as Token Metrics, and subscribe to the trading newsletter.

Managing emotions

Of all the topics in crypto, managing emotions might be the most important. Here are some well-established recommendations for staying steady during trading activity.

- **Sleep:** Don't stay up all night watching crypto price action, even if you have a position. Get 7 to 8 hours of sleep! If you don't get enough sleep, don't trade. Crypto volatility can be stressful, so give your mind and body the opportunity to regenerate.

- **Breathing exercises:** Find guided meditations and breathing exercises that help you relax. An app called Calm is well-known in this arena, but you might also use relaxing music or recordings of nature sounds. If you have the resources, you might get a lot of value out of EnergyforSucess.org.

- **Move your body:** Don't watch Netflix and call it regenerative. Do a few jumping jacks or go for a walk. If you're self-motivated to workout, do it! One of the best crypto traders ever is famous for unwinding by surfing. Find something you enjoy that gets your blood flowing.

- **Eat right:** Forget the Mountain Dew and chips. Your brain needs protein and vegetables. If you trade crypto, you are a financial athlete. Eat like one!

- **Avoid the blame game:** It sounds simplistic, but don't blame yourself if a trade moves against you. Whatever mistakes you made have already been made by the most successful traders out there. Everybody will buy the high and sell the low at some point. Forgive yourself, keep a short memory, and don't dwell on your mistakes.

- Talk to somebody: Find a crypto buddy. Join a good Telegram group chat like the Token Metrics Discussion group. Talk to somebody about your experiences. Crypto traders are participating in the greatest experiment in the history of financial markets, so don't isolate yourself.

Hedging

Hedging is a way of protecting your assets from sharp declines. One of the best ways to understand hedging is to draw a comparison to commodities.

If a farmer produces soybeans, they may want to lock in the price they get for their crop. So if there is a big rally in soybeans, a farmer might use a derivatives instrument to short sell a soybeans futures contract. That way, if news comes out and the price of soybeans drops sharply, the farmer will reap profits from the short sale, and can add that to the price he gets for his crops. The profits from the short sale help the trader make extra money. This is what hedging is all about.

To bring this into the crypto world, suppose you bought Bitcoin at $1,000. If it rises to $13,000 and you suspect Bitcoin is reaching a top, you have two choices. You can sell your Bitcoin and be left with a substantial tax event for capital gains, or if you hedge and use a bitcoin derivative like XBT on BitMEX, you can sell short and profit in case bitcoin drops. If Bitcoin drops to $9,000, you can realize gains on the short trade and retain the psychological peace of mind that comes from holding.

Active portfolio management is necessary in a fast-moving market like crypto. That means buying and passively holding may be difficult if you are new to the game. If you want to hold on for dear life, or HODL, you have to use hedging tactics to protect your crypto holdings during major bear markets. Hedges can be held for a short time or a long time.

Also remember that hedging is a very difficult process. An old Wall Street saying about the difficulty of hedging goes like this: "Hedges are what little doggies pee on."

Supply and demand

Crypto supply and demand can be measured using a volume indicator. Once again, this is both art and science. Volume shows you where most of the price action has traded during the time horizon in question. This shows where buyer demands clash with the sellers' supply.

The high-volume area can indicate whether the bulls or the bears won in the most recent clash. It can also act as a magnet for price.

When a market is highly volatile, it can gravitate back to areas of the most significant volume. If the price drops below a high-volume area, it may continue falling. Understanding supply and demand zones can be critical, mainly when working with intraday charts.

The bottom line

Technical analysis, often referred to as TA, is the study of market price action. Quantitative TA uses algorithms or AI to sense patterns and generate signals. Qualitative technical analysis calls for picking which charts and indicators work for you. We recommend getting your hands on any quant-based tool, like Token Metrics, and subscribe to the trading newsletter.

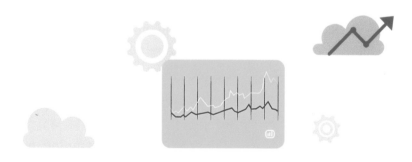

CHAPTER 9

How to Evaluate Crypto Technology

How to Evaluate Crypto Technology

In terms of evaluating the stock market, fundamental analysis combines the performance of stocks with macroeconomic market trends. Cryptocurrencies are unique for their complicated technology and computational methods, so it's necessary to apply fundamental analysis to our evaluation of cryptocurrency.

Our rating models at Token Metrics call for both fundamental and technical analysis to screen the performance of a cryptocurrency. This chapter will guide you through evaluating crypto technology, and how analysis can make a difference in your investing.

The use of cryptographic techniques in blockchain technology guarantees a transaction's security, independent of a central authority, and protection from paying transaction fees twice. The nature of crypto's decentralization, security, and anonymity has made it notorious in the market. A peer-to-peer architecture that supports the transfer of funds and digital assets without a central authority is rather provocative!

This chapter will get technical, but don't be discouraged by it. A basic understanding of the technology behind blockchain and cryptocurrencies will make you a better investor.

A summary of blockchain

Public blockchains operate as decentralized automated systems on a global scale without any central authority. There are millions of contributors (like the developers and the users) who verify the authenticity of transactions on the blockchain. Suppose Alice owes Bob two BTC. If she wants to send him the money, she needs to broadcast that transaction information to miners on the Bitcoin network. The transaction information includes Bob's address and the total amount that Alice will send. She will also include her digital signature and public key.

This lets miners verify that Alice is the actual owner of the BTC being transferred. Miners will confirm the validity of this transaction by inserting the information into a block. To "mine" a block means that nodes on the network pass that block through SHA-256 encryption, which is a cryptographic hashing algorithm created by the National Security Agency.

As the block is mined, miners announce new block information to other miners and verify the transaction's authenticity.

This is a typical example of how transactions are processed on the blockchain. In such a dynamic environment, these publicly shared ledgers need a fair, functional, safe, and reliable mechanism to ensure that all the transactions occurring on the network are genuine — all participants must agree on the status of the ledger. This is what consensus is all about on the blockchain. Consensus mechanisms make sure all nodes synchronize with each other and make sure transactions are acceptable. If they are, then they are added to the blockchain.

With this quick review of blockchain technology complete, let's get into our screening of crypto technology.

Initial screening

The whitepaper

The whitepaper is technical documentation that describes everything about how a project works and what it achieves. It should be clear and specific. The Token Metrics team uses whitepapers to make sure everything is accurately described, up to and including basic information like project roadmaps and a listing of team members.

We focus on the value proposition of the technology, the number of nodes in the network, and the system's architecture.

Blockchain use cases

Governance and payments are two everyday use cases for blockchain technology. Governance can support organizations across different sectors with their network management and help them operate more securely and democratically. Payments (especially within dApps) securely remove the middlemen between two parties who want to transact with each other.

Feasibility

We must see feasibility in the premise behind a given project. If the project makes grandiose or impossible claims, don't bother reviewing the project any further.

Viability

Viability is about seeing how a crypto technology supports the operation of a team and the overall network. To put it as a question: does this company's technology actually help realize your investment goals?

Security attacks

Security can determine the future value of a cryptocurrency. The whitepaper should provide detail on security risks and attack vectors, as well as how these potential vulnerabilities have been mitigated. It's best to only invest in technologies that have been publicly examined by established cryptocurrency auditors. Well-respected crypto auditors include Trail of Bits, OpenZepplin, Certik, and Quantstamp. It's a significant achievement for software to be formally verified. This means the software has been mathematically tested and confirmed to run as designed. Certora is one reputable verification service provider, having verified software for Coinbase, Compound, Aave, Synthetix, and SushiSwap.

Innovation

If initial analysis forms the "first impression" of a cryptocurrency, the next step is to examine the technology through the lens of innovation. Is it doing anything new or important? Innovation is an important differentiator in the crypto market because there are tons of projects in the space, but not all of them can be innovative.

One quick way to determine innovation is to ask if a project is first in its category. Consider that Bitcoin was the first blockchain, Ethereum was the first smart contract blockchain, and so on.

Performance of similar projects

We evaluate past performance of similar projects in the industry to ensure a project doesn't rely on failed or outdated technology. We look at characteristics like volume, market cap, current price, and predicted growth over time.

Practicality

Practical projects are at specific, unique problems. We like projects that go a mile deep and an inch wide to solve them. Conversely, an inch deep and a mile wide is far less practical. No individual crypto project can be everything to everyone.

Total addressable market

"Total addressable market" refers to those who have already joined a project's community and those who will in the future. The bigger the total addressable market, the more desirable the cryptocurrency becomes.

Uniqueness

The project must have some unique quality, like an improved consensus algorithm, for example. Uniqueness demonstrates competitive ideas and methodologies. Projects without original concepts behind them get a negative score here — simple forks or clones of existing projects probably aren't worth your investment.

How to review blockchain architecture

Use cases, technology, and innovation within cryptocurrency varies, but the general system architecture is rather similar. This architecture includes network protocols, transaction protocols, consensus protocols, and internal state.

A blockchain is a type of decentralized ledger. Decentralized ledger technology (DLT) is commonly used in finance because it eliminates the need for a central governing authority. DLT supports enterprises with increased transaction processing efficiency.

Whitepaper

The whitepaper should clearly explain the overall technology, its use case, and its blockchain architecture. While reading, ask questions like:

- Is this a novel idea?

- How does this project compare to other projects?

- Does this project have a future?

Attack resistance

A project's architecture should be resistant to potential attacks. Without a robust architecture, users might be able to spend their cryptocurrencies and then return to clear the transaction history.

This is called "double-spending," and it should be impossible within a reliable blockchain system.

Complexity

Project whitepapers should describe any complex architectures simply and accurately. When a complex architecture is illustrated in a way that's easy to understand, we rank it high on the Token Metrics grading system.

How to review code quality

An independent audit team reviews whether a project's development team has followed best coding practices. This review focuses on the structure of the code, the naming conventions used for the variables, comments in the code, and more.

Open source

Only open source projects are eligible for code review. This kind of software is often produced collaboratively, shared freely, and remains transparent. No company owns or sells the software. This kind of technology production has many far-reaching benefits, not the least of which is that we get to look under the hood at how it works.

Programming language

The Token Metrics research team likes to see projects use the most appropriate programming language for implementing their particular idea. We like to see projects use C++, Rust, Erlang, Ruby, Go, and Solidity. It's a red flag to see a project designed in an outdated language.

Lines of code

We look at the number of lines of code in a project's repository, excluding any third-party libraries or code forked from another repository. These numbers are readily available on any public Github.

Code commits per month

We expect to see a certain amount of activity on Github or other open source code repositories each month. If we don't see it, then we score them negatively. When a project has regular new code commits on its public repository, it means the team is working hard. If it has no recent commits, say six months or longer, it might mean the project is abandoned or has very little support. That makes it a riskier investment.

Quality of code

Every developer writes code, but it's impressive when code quality stands out among the rest. We inspect the quality of code in terms of programming languages used, overall technical architecture, repository format and structure, and the technical specification of the source code.

Code comments

We look for code comments at the file level or function level, as well as any project level documentation that provides clear instructions or how-tos.

Test coverage

The overall test coverage is significant for ensuring that the project team spends enough time checking the quality of its source code. We expect to see a certain level of unit tests and integration test coverage. Unit tests are checks on individual components of software that make sure they function as intended. Integration tests are for groups of components to see if they work cohesively together as intended.

Maintainability index

The maintainability index is a metric that measures how easy it is to support and change a project's source code. The index is scored on a scale of 0 to 100. The higher the score, the more maintainable the code. A range between 20 and 100 is considered to be in the "green zone," or having good maintainability. Projects need to have high maintainability because it should be easy to fix the inevitable bugs that emerge along the way.

Roadmap

A roadmap provides details on the actual development of a project. We rely on the roadmap and any progress made to determine whether the project will deliver a fully functional product within its stipulated time frame. Projects that have no product roadmap, or just a proof of concept, get penalized. It might take a while for them to launch their product, which adds additional investment risk.

Usability for infrastructure projects

Often touted as a significant advantage of distributed ledger technology, the usability of infrastructure projects also poses significant challenges and comes with certain responsibilities. Users must store complex private keys in order to manage their funds safely. Seed phrases are lists of words that store all the information necessary to recover crypto funds on-chain, and losing any part of that list can mean losing your funds forever. But this never happens with traditional repositories.

This calls for a better solution for bringing legal users into the digital asset ecosystem. This might be an Application Programming Interface (API) or software development kit (SDK).

APIs define interactions between multiple software intermediaries. In the blockchain paradigm, these different intermediaries are the nodes of the network. APIs define the calls or requests made, how they're made, and the data involved for each.

Dynamic APIs bridge traditional finance with digital finance.

SDKs are a combination of software development tools for a developer to code, test, compile, and publish software. Projects that invite developers to build applications on top of them using their APIs and SDKs are more desirable. They provide more usability and sustainable long-term value by laying the foundation for a full-fledged ecosystem to bloom.

Ease of use

The project must be easy to use for its intended audience, and complicated blockchain technology must be hidden from the regular user whenever possible. People should be able to use these products without being deep blockchain experts.

Team

Team structure is essential for evaluating that team's crypto technology. We look for active developers with relevant coding skills.

Active developers

The number of active developers, or people who have developed on a team's Github in the last two weeks, is an important data point.

We consider a team with over three active developers to have a good performance. The project needs continuous progress.

Developer's open source history

We look for each developer's Github account or other open source activities to categorize them as a junior, senior, or expert developer. Having active developers with many years of open source contribution history is a significant plus.

Developer's coding style

We are interested in developers' coding styles. They should follow best practices for writing readable, maintainable code.

References

We like to see links to all the references used for any research. This usually includes links to project websites, whitepapers, and other resources.

The bottom line

Proper evaluation of crypto projects helps you avoid scams, reduce loss, and minimize the risk associated with investing in cryptocurrencies.

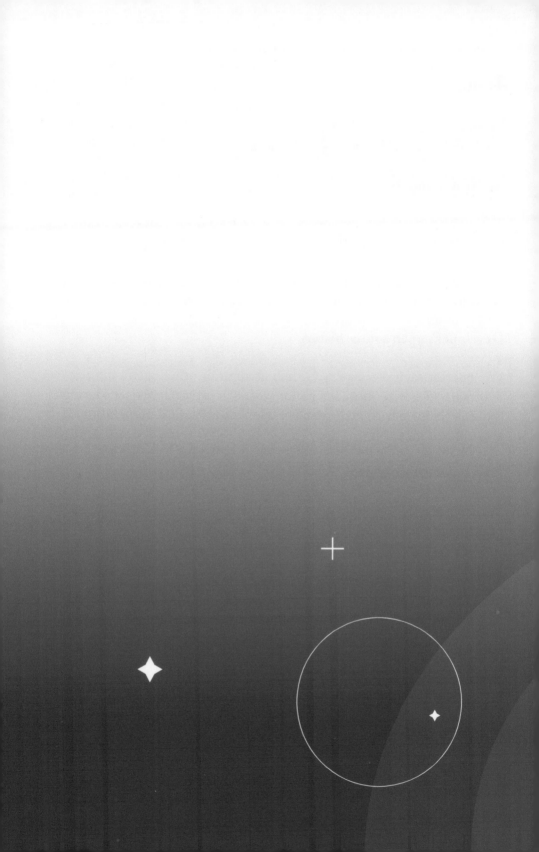

CHAPTER 10

Introduction to Token Sales:
ICOs, IEOs, and IDOs

Introduction to Token Sales: ICOs, IEOs, and IDOs

What are token sales?

A token sale is a limited period of time during which a set number of tokens are made available for purchase to the public. They might exchange established cryptocurrencies like Bitcoin, Ethereum, or major stablecoins to acquire these new tokens.

A token sale can be compared to an IPO on the stock market. An IPO is when shares of a company's stock are offered for sale to the public as a form of fundraising for the company. Similarly, a token sale raises money for a crypto project. But there are some crucial differences between an IPO and the various flavors of token sales, which we will address below.

What are Initial Coin Offerings (ICOs)?

ICOs are a kind of crowdfunding for the crypto world. Blockchain startups offer investors the opportunity to invest in their projects by purchasing some of their cryptocurrency in advance. In exchange for financing the project, investors receive digital tokens at a low purchase price.

Investors expect the value of their tokens to rise over time so they can sell them at a higher price than they first bought them for. ICOs typically take place in the early phases of a project, and the project leadership uses those funds to continue developing their products.

Suppose a blockchain startup creates a new product on the Ethereum blockchain. They determine the value of their product based on what they think it's worth, as well as how much money they need to fundraise in order to scale effectively. But this value does not remain fixed: it changes according to the dynamics of the market. Token sales are very decentralized in this sense, letting market supply and demand (as opposed to some central authority) set the price. The project determines the ICO's initial price at the time of launch, and the price increases or decreases based on demand.

Let's imagine a Netflix competitor called Webflix. Webflix does everything Netflix does, except it's open source and decentralized without any central authority controlling it. The data moves in a peer-to-peer fashion, similar to BitTorrent.

Webflix membership can only be purchased using tokens called Flix Coins. In order to raise money for operating Webflix, we sell these tokens to the public ahead of launch. People will buy them because they expect to resell the tokens for a higher value, or trade them for membership at Webflix. But this only works if our project takes off. If not, the users end up with a bunch of worthless tokens.

ICOs take the best from IPOs and crowdfunding, creating a decentralized system with no central authority or middleman involved.

What are Initial Exchange Offerings (IEOs)?

An initial exchange offering is a byproduct of the ICO. IEOs strive to be more secure by adding curation to the offering. IEOs are underwritten and take place on a cryptocurrency exchange like Binance or Coinlist. In this scenario, the crypto exchange works as a middleman between the investor and the company raising money. Thus, the exchange is responsible for vetting the project, marketing the project, and selling the tokens for a fee.

Although IEOs provide more security and curation, they are still a high-risk investment and should be considered cautiously. At the present moment, the best IEO platforms from the perspective of return on investment are Coinlist and Binance Launchpad.

What are Initial DEX Offerings (IDOs)?

IDOs are like IEOs, but they take place on a decentralized exchange

(DEX). IDOs are quickly becoming the preferred method for launching a token to raise capital for crypto projects, as they merge ICOs and IEOs.

IDOs are new to the market, however, and are less established than other fundraising mechanisms, but they solve the issue of depending on centralized platforms.

IEOs and IDOs are largely the same, except for the platform that hosts the fundraising process. The former is centralized (Binance, CoinList) and the latter is decentralized (Polkastarter).

What are Initial Public Offerings (IPOs)?

An IPO is what happens when a company goes from private to public by selling shares of its stock on the public market. Companies go public to raise funds and gain liquidity. They might reinvest this capital in their infrastructure or scale the company.

The IPO process isn't very democratic. It favors large institutional investors, like hedge funds and large banks.

What is crowdfunding?

Crowdfunding is the practice of raising small amounts of money from a large number of people. By getting the word out on social media and leveraging crowdfunding websites like Kickstarter, entrepreneurs can expand their pool of investors beyond the usual venture capitalists and angel investors.

How crypto is disrupting venture capital

The traditional way of raising money for a startup involves creating a business plan, getting multiple rounds of funding, and eventually reaching a profitable exit. But the proliferation of cryptocurrencies has led to the development of alternative financing methods.

Token sales provide funding to a startup for developing and launching their product while incentivizing the community to invest in it. Entrepreneurs here don't have to go through rounds of deals and negotiations. If the project succeeds and your tokens increase in value, you can sell them for a profit. In 2017 alone, the top 15 token sales raised over $100 million.

But things can get a little tricky when it comes to token sales since there's no real-world market value to discuss. This can lead to volatile price changes, and that kind of risk might dissuade an old-school investor from participating. But savvy investors see this as an opportunity: they don't have to wait for an IPO to recover their investment and make a profit. Early investors could quickly recoup their initial investment when a project launches, as well as make significant profits if the project has high value and demand.

The history of ICOs

Token sales have come a long way since their first appearance in 2013. Ethereum, Bitcoin's biggest competitor, had one of the most successful token sales in crypto history, raising $18 million at $0.311 per token. Ethereum currently has a market cap that's well over $156 billion at the time of writing. It's cemented itself as one of the best crypto investments you could've participated in.

But the history of ICOs is not all sunshine and rainbows. One tragic example of an ICOs gone wrong is the Decentralized Autonomous Organization, or DAO. The DAO was an Ethereum-based company that wanted to build a model for an organization that would intelligently and efficiently allocate capital. The company raised more than $180 million over just a couple of months, but due to a glitch in the software, hackers made away with more than $50 million. This destroyed the DAO project and sent Ethereum into crisis mode.

Is it safe to invest in an ICO?

You can make a great deal of money investing in token sales, but you can just as easily lose it.

Token sales are a high-risk-high-reward investment, and as with any investment, you can't really predict success with absolute certainty.

Companies might not complete the project, or might even maliciously trick you into investing in their business without any intention of ever launching. This should be expected for an entirely new and mostly unregulated field. However, you can take a few measures to assess the credibility of an ICO project to avoid getting scammed:

- **Beware of anonymous teams.** If the project developers are anonymous or unknown to anyone in the community, that's a red flag. If they are not willing to put their reputation on the line, it might be best to keep your money. Alternatively, wait until the community has audited the project's code and some early success or traction once the token starts trading.

- **Only invest in IEOs on reputable exchanges.** The crypto community has managed to regulate ICOs through IEOs. An exchange puts its reputation on the line to screen various companies, only offering the most promising ones for investment.

- **Be skeptical of lofty goals.** If the developers set unrealistic goals for what they want to achieve, they might not know what they're doing. Perhaps worse, they might not care and are just looking for a way to scam a quick buck out of you.

- **Avoid projects without a functioning product.** Legitimate blockchain projects typically have already built a functioning product that's available to their users. If a project doesn't have a functional product, it's a precarious investment! You are essentially investing in an idea.

The economics of how a token is used within a blockchain ecosystem is vital. Suppose the token being sold doesn't capture value or incentivize investors to hold it. In that case, it is probably a useless token and likely going to go to zero.

Token auctions (reverse Dutch auction)

Token auctions, also known as reverse Dutch auctions, are another kind of crypto investment vehicle. This kind of auction operates backwards from the norm: it starts at an extremely high price and market cap that slowly decreases.

Investors will typically wait until they see an acceptable price, then purchase tokens at that price. Investors can save money by waiting and watching the price go lower, but these tokens have a reserve price. Once it reaches the reserve, the sale will end.

The best approach here is to go in with a pre-determined price you are willing to pay as an investor, and once the token drops to that price, invest. But if it hits its reserve price and
the sale closes before you can invest, then don't worry: you just avoided an investment that probably wasn't right for you.

The different stages of token sales

Seed round

The seed round is often not very public, as it's the earliest stage of investment. The project's goal at this time is to raise money from venture capital firms or a network of family and friends.

These early investors usually get the token at a discounted price, making maximum profits when the token reaches exchanges. The only problem is that a company's token might not make it to exchanges.

This makes the seed round a high-risk stage of investment. It should only be done with trusted projects. Seed rounds are usually only available to accredited investors, who are people with a net worth exceeding $1 million or an annual income exceeding $200,000.

Private sales

Projects at the private sale stage have things like a whitepaper and website ready to go. They've built some degree of community around their product. But there is still little visibility into its workings, so people who participate here are often tipped into it by other investors in their network. This stage is also risky, as some projects will not succeed.

Public pre-sale

At this stage, a company has secured funding and is ready to roll out the marketing for its token sale. This stage is an opportunity for people to invest in projects at a discounted price. A public pre-sale is similar to a private sale, but it's marketed publicly to the community members and usually has a low minimum investment requirement.

Public token sale whitelist

Some projects leave allocations for their community members. This phase often has a time window ranging from a couple days to a couple weeks. The team members usually do a lot of marketing at this stage, asking community members to whitelist (subscribe to the token sale in advance) to show interest. Most times, only those on the whitelist and other approved individuals get to participate.

Public token sale

This is the point when the token sale actually takes place. At this stage, marketing momentum has reached a climax and whitelisted community members can participate at a higher price (compared to pre-sales or private sales). Although there is no further discount on the price, investors can still profit when the projects launch on exchanges and the tokens gain value.

How to invest in token sales

Token Metrics helps share interesting projects with our customers via our daily newsletter and YouTube channel. When you find something you want to invest in, go to the project's site and do some research — make sure it's a legitimate business. Read the whitepaper and make sure it includes a description of the project, its real-world applications, a set of realistic goals, and a clear roadmap of how the idea becomes a product. Then gauge community opinion on the project. Browse social media and check relevant Telegram channels to see what kind of sentiment the project is attracting. You might search the name of the project along with keywords like "scam," "con," or "MLM." If you see any posts that credibly include these keywords, that's a potential red flag.

Once you've found a token sale that passes muster with you, get in on their seed round, private sale, or public sale by reaching out to the team or following any public registration instructions. If it's an IEO, you will need to use tokens pertaining to the exchange where the IEO is happening, like BNB for Binance, KCS for Kucoin, and so on. If it's an IDO, you will need to hold a minimum number of tokens to participate. For example, you must hold a minimum of 3,000 Polkastarter for a certain number of days in order to participate in their sales.

Once the payment is made and the token sale or IEO is over, store your new tokens in a hardware wallet like a Nano Ledger or Trezor. If there's no supported hardware wallet option, make sure you use two-factor authentication and a strong, unique password on your exchange account.

After the estimated project listing deadline has elapsed, the tokens get listed on crypto exchanges like Kucoin, Huobi, or OKEX, and they're then available to buy and sell to the general public.

The bottom line

ICOs, IEOs, and IDOs are fundraising tools. IEOs are quite like ICOs, but with an added layer of screening by reputable exchanges that lower the risk involved. IDOs are like IEOs, but they're decentralized. Do your due diligence by researching the project before investing in it!

CHAPTER 11

Introduction to Security Tokens

CHAPTER 11

Introduction to Security Tokens

What are security tokens?

Security tokens are a digital representation of a real-world asset. Security tokens might also be called digital securities, smart securities, programmable securities, or crypto securities. They are changing the status quo of capital markets by moving toward an architecture built on distributed ledger technology. A security token can come in the form of equity, debt, hybrids, or derivatives.

Unlike utility tokens, security tokens have intrinsic value and real-life use cases.

Providing liquidity to illiquid securities

The tokenization of non-liquid assets like fine art, precious metals, sports teams, real estate, and more could change the way investors value and think about their investments. Instead of owning a painting by Monet, for example, you might invest $2,000 in a $200 million Monet fund attached to several of his works. The same goes for a $35 million mansion in Beverly Hills — you might gain fractional ownership with a smaller investment, earning yourself the according portion of any rent that's paid there.

Tokenization lets regular people diversify their investment portfolios in unprecedented ways.

Opening up capital markets globally

Security token offerings (STOs) are an opportunity to provide quick, easy, and affordable access to a broad investor market. STOs only call for an internet connection to allow for investing as you wish. Their exposure to capital markets will grow immensely and create an economy where people can have their money work for them.

24/7 trading on secondary markets

The world's stock markets are only open for six or seven hours during the weekdays. Companies often take advantage of this schedule and release impactful information outside of those hours.

But security tokens can be traded 24/7 on secondary markets, creating unprecedented liquidity. For example, you could automate dividends and voting rights using the programmable aspect of security tokens. You could also increase dividends and voting rights for investors that held a stock for longer than five years, incentivizing them to keep the shares for extended periods.

The possibilities are endless.

Smart contracts will replace middlemen

Smart contracts are on their way to replacing lawyers and arbitrators for standardizing and automating contractual obligations. Third parties that initiate or approve agreements will no longer be necessary — the algorithm determines the time to fulfill and automate payments.

What are securities?

Securities are tradable financial instruments

The legal definition of a "security" varies significantly between countries, but it is generally defined as a tradable financial instrument that derives its value from another asset.

In 1946, the Supreme Court saw the case of the SEC vs. W.J. Howey Co. This monumental case established the so-called "Howey test," which is used to this day to determine what is and isn't a security.

Securities are tradable financial instruments

The legal definition of a "security" varies significantly between countries, but it is generally defined as a tradable financial instrument that derives its value from another asset. In 1946, the Supreme Court saw the case of the SEC vs. W.J. Howey Co. This monumental case established the so-called "Howey test," which is used to this day to determine what is and isn't a security.

Howey Co. was a citrus farm in Florida that decided to lease out half of its extensive property in order to finance additional development. The land was sold to speculators who had none of the knowledge, skills, or equipment to care for citrus trees. The land was leased on the assumption that it would generate profit if it was cared for by an expert. Howey Co. sidestepped the law when it failed to register these transactions with the U.S Securities and Exchange Commission. The case was appealed all the way to the Supreme Court.

The Supreme Court found that the Howey Co. transactions constituted investment contracts. They were not only offering simple interest, but also further opportunities for money-making and profit-sharing.

Transactions are considered investment contracts if they fulfill the following criteria:

- An investment of money is involved.

- The investment is in a typical enterprise.

- There is an assumption of profit to be made.

In 2018, the SEC ruled that Bitcoin and Ethereum are not securities. The main argument was that because the two platforms are decentralized, investors do not rely on third parties to profit. Although the news came as a great relief to the crypto community, SEC officials claim that some ICOs might be declared securities. They would have to follow the same regulations as stocks, meaning that they would have certain reporting requirements for protecting investors and the market's integrity.

Who creates securities?

There are a number of ways to create a security, but they all have an issuer. The issuer can be a company raising funds for future expansion, like a company issuing stock via IPO. It can also be a governmental organization, like the treasury, taking on debt by selling bonds on the market.

A security transaction is completed after the issuer sets the terms for their specific security. The investor pays the requested amount, and gains ownership of the security.

What are private and public securities?

When an issuer and an investor trade a security without the help of a publicly available market, like the stock market, they are dealing in private securities. These are commonly shares of stock issued by a privately held company. Gaining access to this type of security could be difficult, and they are significantly less liquid than public securities. The lack of large, public secondary markets makes finding a trading partner increasingly difficult.

Public securities are financial instruments listed on public markets like the New York Stock Exchange. The existence of large liquid secondary markets makes finding a trading partner relatively easy. But issuing securities on the public market is highly restricted, and companies must first fulfill a lengthy list of regulatory requirements.

What are shareholder rights?

By law, securities give their owners certain rights. These can be economic rights, control rights, information rights, litigation rights, or even physical delivery rights for commodity derivatives.

Let's take a closer look at each of these.

What are economic rights?

Economic rights differ depending on if a financial instrument is an equity, debt, or both.

When it comes to equities, investors have the economic right to receive part of the profits by receiving paid dividends.

On the other hand, if the owner of a security receives a fixed income regardless of the issuer's profitability, then the security is debt-like. If the security has equity and debt characteristics, like revenue participation notes and preferred stock, we refer to it as a quasi-equity or a hybrid.

What are control rights?

Investors might want to retain a certain amount of control over management and the general direction of the company. Equity owners may have the right to participate and vote on matters in shareholder meetings. Some companies choose to have multiple kinds of stock with different voting rights for each.

A common stock gives one shareholder the right of one vote and a proportion of the dividends, depending on the total number of shares he or she holds. But early founders often issue dual shares to preserve control of the company over later-stage investors.

Dual share class stocks are often called Class A and Class B, representing the varying control rights for each. Google is an excellent example of a company with multiple publicly traded stocks. In 2014, Google split its stock and created an A class and a C class.

The reason was simple: the founders wanted to retain as much control over the company as possible. Although the difference in price between the two was relatively small, there was one crucial distinction: voting rights.

The company's class C shares (GOOG) came without voting rights, while class A shares (GOOGL) had one voting right.

What are information rights?

Depending on the jurisdiction and type of Security, the issuer must disclose certain information to existing or future investors.

1. Privately held securities
Privately held securities are not as strict as publicly listed securities, but the company must report specific details of its operations to its shareholders. Annual reports, like audited financial statements and the cap table (shareholder registry), are examples of the type of information these records must contain.

2. Listed securities
When issuing a public security, companies must also file a document called a prospectus that contains all relevant information and disclosures with the SEC. Investors can use this document to make an educated decision on investing.

Once the security is publicly traded, the issuer must provide quarterly and annual financial reports, a profit warning, and any information that might affect the security's price. All these measures serve to keep investors informed while preventing insider trading.

3. Litigation rights
Shareholders play an essential role in the governance of a company. They each own a small portion of it, and they have the right to affect change within the company. When it comes to equity instruments, litigation usually happens after an investor registers a loss from buying or selling shares based on false information from management. If the investors decide to start a civil action against the company to recover said losses, they will file a derivative suit.

4. Physical delivery rights
As far as futures and options contracts go, one of the parties promises the delivery of an underlying asset on an agreed future date.

The other party therefore has the right to physical delivery, a right that's exclusive to commodity derivatives.

How are securities regulated?

The regulator's goal is to ensure a safe environment for all market participants. They certify that the company's information is factually correct and that investors get fair treatment. Regulations limit who can sell, invest, give advice, and exchange securities.

Who can buy and sell securities?

Large institutions and accredited investors, like banks and high-net-worth individuals, are the usual suspects in the US.

In the European Union, a country's specific regulatory agency must approve who can interact with securities. A broker or trader here must be accredited by the relevant authority and be part of an investment firm. That investment firm also needs to fulfill certain requirements with the proper regulatory agency.

A broker-dealer in the US needs to register with the SEC and join a "self-regulatory organization" before being allowed to sell securities. Financial service companies in the UK need to register with the Financial Conduct Authority (FCA).

Who can run a marketplace or exchange?

Higher speeds and lower costs have made Multilateral Trading Facilities (MTFs) the norm in the EU. An excellent example of an MTF is the UK's LMAX Exchange, which offers spot foreign currency exchange and precious metals trading.

MTFs must be licensed by the relevant authority. For example, the FCA issues the license for LMAX.

Like MTFs, the United States has Alternative Trading Systems (ATS), which are mostly regulated as broker-dealers, and are licensed by the US SEC.

USA security regulations

Under the Security Act of 1993, security tokens in the USA need to adhere to four specific regulations: Regulation D, Regulation A+, Regulation CF, and Regulation S. We'll unpack each of these below.

Regulation D

The security issuer must fill out Form D when a security is sold. The issuer can publicly advertise his offering in compliance with Section 506C, which states that only accredited investors are allowed to participate, and all information provided in the offering must be "free from false or misleading statements."

An accredited investor has a special status and can invest in securities that aren't registered with financial authorities. This privilege is given to individuals or entities that satisfy certain net worth or income requirements. Accredited investors must meet one or more of these conditions:

- An annual income of at least $200,000, or a joint household income of $300,000 for the last two years. Expectation of future earnings must be at least the same.

- A net worth exceeding $1 million, excluding the value of the primary residence. This figure can be attained individually or jointly with a spouse.

- A business entity can be an accredited investor if it holds more than $5 million in assets.

Regulation A+ (Mini-IPO)

This exemption takes a lot of time and is more expensive than other options, but lets the issuer gain SEC approval. The security can be offered to non-accredited investors through a general solicitation for up to $50 million in investment.

Regulation CF

This regulation lets eligible companies offer securities for sale through crowdfunding.

The rules:

- Require all transactions under Regulation Crowdfunding to take place online through an SEC-registered intermediary, either a broker-dealer or a funding portal.

- Permit a company to raise a maximum amount of $1,070,000 through crowdfunding within a 12-month period.

- Limit the amount that individual investors can invest across all crowdfunding offerings within a 12-month period.

- Require disclosure of information to investors and intermediaries in filings with the SEC.

Securities purchased in a crowdfunding transaction usually cannot be resold for one year.

Regulation S

This regulation is for offerings outside the US, and registration is not required, as mentioned under section 5 of the 1033 Act. The issuer must follow the guidelines and regulations of the country where the security is being offered.

What are security tokens?

Security tokens are digital representations of proof of ownership. If you own the token, you own the underlying asset as well. These tokens give you the right to receive profits and offer similar advantages as general cryptocurrencies.

Some of these advantages include:

- Reduced friction for easy trading over the internet.

- The opportunity to implement smart contracts and eliminate third parties from a transaction.

- Easy divisibility, as assets can be split into smaller pieces for investors to share.

Security tokens are subject to regulations the same way as stocks, bonds, and other securities. Furthermore, if someone steals your security token, you are legally entitled to have it reinstated to you.

What are security token offerings (STOs)?

Security token offerings are quite comparable to an IPO. The primary difference is in the distribution (STOs happen online) and the subsequent location of the secondary market (they work globally). An STO is also significantly cheaper than an IPO when it's carried out under regulatory frameworks like Regulation D, S, or A+.

Regulations protect investors participating in an STO by granting them economic control, information rights, rights litigation, and physical delivery rights. An organization can legally provide tokens to buyers with benefits like dividend payment, profit sharing, and voting rights. A security token can retain the attributes of a utility token when it's used for native transactions in an organization's service or product.

Where to trade security tokens?

tZero

Online retailer Overstock launched a subsidiary called tZERO at the beginning of 2019. tZERO is the first licensed blockchain-enabled alternative trading system where investors can trade security tokens. It's a cost-effective service that includes token issuance, management, and trading solutions. Issuers save vast amounts of money on their research and regulatory costs. tZERO integrates regulations directly in the token creation protocol.

tZERO has raised $270 million at a $1.5 billion valuation, and issues tokens per SEC regulations. Token holders receive a 10% dividend of adjusted gross revenue quarterly, after meeting the conditions mentioned in the offering memorandum and being approved by the board.

OpenFinance

OpenFinance offers a regulated trading platform for alternative digital assets and token-based securities. They've developed a streamlined, compliant process for secondary market trading.

Security token issuance platforms

Securitize

Securitize is a platform that enables compliant digital securities liquidity and insurance on the blockchain. Issuers can use the platform to manage their digital securities. Its smart contracts are designed to support token information on the Ethereum blockchain.

Polymath

What Ethereum is to ICOs, Polymath wants to be for security tokens. Polymath has developed its ST-20 token standard on top of Ethereum. Polymath's platform offers legal and technical solutions for tokenizing stocks, bonds, or any other asset on the blockchain. It uses its native POLY token for all economic operations.

Harbor

Harbor is an all-encompassing blockchain platform for digital securities.

It uses an Ethereum-based permission token called R-Token for transfers, only when approved by a SEC-compliant on-chain regulator service. It offers liquid investment opportunities and makes it easy to tokenize an existing company's shares of stock.

Where to find STOs

SharesPost

With 250 private company partners and $4.5 billion in transactions, the SharesPost marketplace is a handy tool for researching and trading traditional and digital securities of private growth companies.

STO Market

If you are looking for a directory of security token offerings, then STO Market is for you. With partners like Securitize and Polymath, the site has a firm grip on what's going on in the STO market.

Bank to the Future

Bank to the Future is a global investment platform that can only be accessed by professional investors with an annual income over $200,000 who are willing to invest at least $1,000 every year.

Possible concerns with security tokens

ICOs have been doing their utmost best to avoid being classified as a security, and for excellent reasons. ICOs depend heavily on creating a network effect to foster a community. Restrictions on who can invest and how the tokens can be exchanged can severely hinder projects from creating a robust community.

STOs are not as dependent on network effects. Fewer investors, exchanges, and a more negligible network effect will negatively influence STO liquidity on secondary markets. Filing paperwork with any authority hurts decentralization. So instead of allowing security tokens to reach their full decentralized potential, this technology will be limited to being just an iteration of traditional securities.

Instead of fast and wild profits, returns will be calmer and more expected. If you don't feel like engaging in the risk-reward system, the argument is that you should undertake a public offering in some jurisdiction. However, STOs can attract institutional investors while we work toward complete decentralization.

The bottom line

Security tokens represent real assets and real money. This new technology will bring never-before-seen liquidity to illiquid securities and open up the entire world's capital markets. They seem to be the next logical step after the bubbles within Bitcoin, utility tokens, and DeFi.

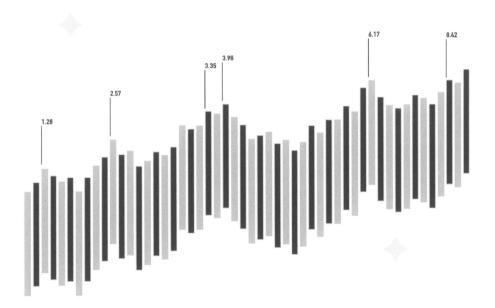

CHAPTER 12

Introduction to Decentralized Finance (DeFi)

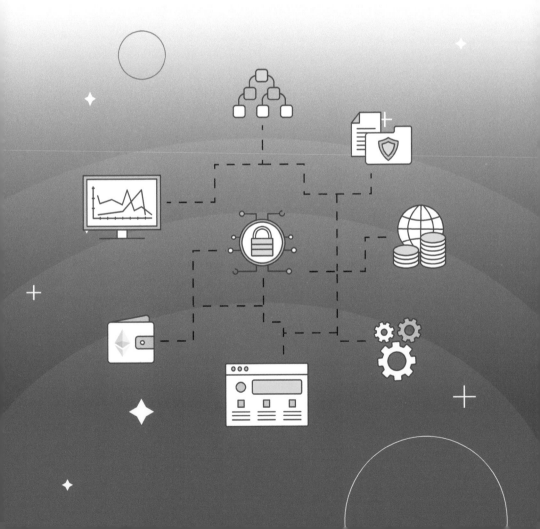

Introduction to Decentralized Finance (DeFi)

What is DeFi?

In traditional banking, lenders and borrowers are legally required to know each others' identities, and the lender assesses a borrower's ability to pay back the debt. DeFi turns this paradigm on its head for maximum privacy. According to DeFi Llama, a site that tracks and analyzes decentralized finance protocols, DeFi has currently captured over $100 billion in total value. It's a force to be reckoned with!

Defining DeFi

DeFi was first introduced by Brendan Forster, co-founder, and CTO of Dharma Labs, in his 2018 article "Announcing De.Fi, A Community for Decentralized Finance Platforms."

DeFi refers to a broad category of financial applications built on top of open, trust-minimized, programmable, and censorship-resistant networks. These applications further the legacy financial system, or design entirely new use cases. DeFi fundamentally involves a brand-new monetary system built on public blockchains. The vision is to let anyone transact as they see fit from anywhere in the world.

Differences between DeFi dApps and traditional financial intermediaries

- **Interoperability** – DeFi products can fit together like Lego pieces to develop new and innovative use cases. Things like decentralized exchanges, stablecoins, and prediction markets can be combined to create entirely new products.

- **Permissionless** – Anyone is permitted to join in and participate. There is no intermediary preventing you from transacting.

- **No humans involved** – The rules governing a DeFi application are written as a smart contract and deployed to the blockchain, where they are executed as computer code.

- **Transparency** – Anyone can audit the code that makes a DeFi app work. This builds trust with users, as they can dig in to understand the software's functions.

- **Global** – dApps can be accessed no matter where the user is. Although local regulations may vary, most DeFi apps are available to everyone everywhere.

- **Flexibility in user experience** – Unlike traditional banking, you do not need to go to a physical building. You are your bank.

DeFi platforms

MakerDAO

MakerDAO is one of the most significant DeFi applications on Ethereum. The open source project lets developers create DAI stablecoins that are pegged to the US dollar by overcollateralizing their digital assets. The total value locked in Maker currently exceeds $9.7 billion.

DAI satisfies the four functions of money:

- A store of value.

- A medium of exchange.

- A unit of account.

- A standard of deferred payment.

Synthetix

Synthetix is a protocol that lets users create and exchange synthetic versions of assets like silver or gold, and traditional currencies like the British pound or US dollar. It trades on the Ethereum blockchain, and it currently has some $1.85 billion of total value locked.

These collateral assets, called synthetics, are backed by the platform's Ethereum-based SNX token. Synthetics can simulate real-world financial assets and track their value.

Compound

Compound is a decentralized protocol for money markets on the Ethereum blockchain. It is a blockchain-based borrowing and lending dApp, meaning you can lend your crypto out to others and earn interest on it.

The total value locked at the time of this writing is $9.02 billion. Anyone can supply assets to Compound's liquidity pool to start earning interest. Those interest rates algorithmically adjust based on supply and demand.

The Compound protocol sets aside 10% of interest paid as reserves and the rest goes to suppliers. A token called cToken represents the users' balances.

How to use DeFi

To get started with DeFi, you need to get a wallet that supports Ethereum. A common choice is MetaMask, a browser extension created for interacting with Web3 applications — decentralized applications running on a blockchain.

The main categories of DeFi protocols are lending, borrowing, stablecoin, and exchange protocols. You might want to get started by lending out your cryptocurrencies. Use yearn.finance to search for the best deal — it aggregates them all in one place. You could become a yield farmer by earning governance tokens as a reward for lending out your cryptocurrencies.

You might also deposit your funds in a decentralized exchange like Uniswap, earning fees as a market maker.

You could also experiment with elastic supply cryptocurrencies like Ampleforth. The token supply "rebases" daily, meaning the supply increases or decreases algorithmically in order to hit a target price.

Be careful going down the DeFi rabbit hole. This is a highly experimental and risky space within crypto, so do your research before interacting with any dApp.

DeFi lending and borrowing

DeFi lets individuals lend money to others and earn interest without a third party involved. For the borrower, DeFi grants access to loans in a faster, more convenient way than traditional banking systems allow.

Smart contracts ensure the interest rate and other necessary information gets programmed into the lending agreements. The lending interest rates vary across tokens and platforms, and they depend on the supply and demand for loans. If the market has a higher demand for loans, the interest rate increases, while a higher supply of loans decreases the interest rate.

Let's examine some common questions people have here.

Question 1: How do you check the borrower's credibility and make sure they'll pay back a loan?

Before the borrowers can receive loans, they need to deposit their collateral assets ahead of time into a smart contract. The lenders hold that collateral there. If the borrower cannot pay back the loans, the borrower's collateral is released to the lender.

Question 2: What if the value of the collateral decreases?

Under such circumstances, borrowers are unwilling to pay back their loans, since their collateral isn't as valuable anymore. When the value of the collateral decreases, the lender usually loses money.

DeFi platforms use liquidation to solve this problem. Once the collateral value can no longer cover the loan, the platform liquidates that collateral, selling it to repay the loans in full to the lenders.

Money market protocols

What are DeFi money markets?

Money markets in decentralized finance (DeFi) are markets in which anyone can lend or borrow crypto assets. This provides a mechanism in which idle assets can be used productively to earn interest. The interest earned by an asset is algorithmically determined based on how many people supply and borrow the asset.

DeFi money markets are fully non-custodial, meaning the lender can withdraw his assets and accrued interest whenever necessary without waiting for the loan to mature, quite unlike traditional lending products.

How money market protocols work

In DeFi, money market protocols store liquid crypto assets in a pool where the interest rates are derived algorithmically, depending on the supply and demand for a particular asset. Lenders and borrowers pay a floating interest rate instead of a loan with a specified maturity or interest rate. Money markets on the Ethereum blockchain are peer-to-peer, meaning anyone can lend their liquid crypto assets to an anonymous borrower. Lenders deposit an ERC-20 token asset into a money market pool and receive an interest-bearing token in exchange.

Suppose a lender deploys 10 ETH to the ETH Compound money market, where they will receive 10 interest-bearing cETH tokens that are redeemable for ETH at any point (Figure 12.2). Interest-bearing tokens and floating interest rates let lenders withdraw without waiting for a loan to reach maturity.

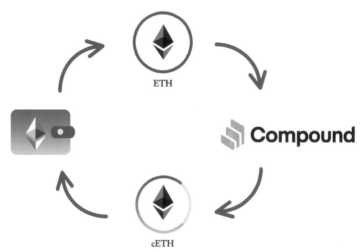

Figure 12.2: An example of a money market pool

Flash loans & DeFi arbitrage

Flash loans are a novel category of loans that are enabled by cryptographic proofs. These loans require no collateral, as the loan and repayments are settled in a single transaction. The purpose of this type of loan is to let individuals with small amounts of capital borrow large quantities of crypto assets, often for complex arbitrage opportunities across the DeFi ecosystem.

Consider the example of when the DAI stablecoin significantly deviated from its $1 peg, sitting at $0.90 on one exchange and $0.99 on another. A trader would borrow USDC from Aave via a flash loan, then purchase the $0.90 DAI to sell it at $0.99 on the other exchange. The USDC loan and its repayment are settled in the same transaction. If the transaction is reverted, the individual will only incur gas fees, and the flash loan will not be executed.

Decentralized exchanges and aggregators

What are decentralized exchanges?

Decentralized exchanges (DEX) are core DeFi infrastructure that provide trading services to users without deposits or loss of custody of their crypto assets. Instead of transferring assets to a centralized exchange, users can simply connect their wallets to decentralized exchanges and remain in full control of their assets. At its base level, a decentralized exchange is a permissionless smart contract, so anyone can access these trading services anywhere in the world, at any time they want.

How do decentralized exchanges work?

Most popular decentralized exchanges operate on the key innovation called automated market makers (AMMs), which determine an asset's pricing for spot trading based on the relative amounts of liquidity available in a trading pairs liquidity pool.

Liquidity pool: A smart contract that stores crypto assets, usually in a binary pair. For example, ETH/USDC.

Automated market maker: A mathematical equation that determines the price of a trade based on the relative share of assets of the binary trading pair in the liquidity pool.

The most common AMM, pioneered by Bancor and then by Uniswap, is the constant-product AMM shown in Equation 12.1

$$\textit{Equation 12.1:} X^*Y = K$$

X represents the quantity of reserve token 1, and Y represents the quantity of reserve token 2. K is the product of both reserve quantities.

Suppose Bob wants to purchase 10 ETH using the USDC in his Metamask wallet. A Uniswap spot trade simply deposits the USDC into the liquidity pool and removes ETH from the pool. But as the trade size increases, this trade doesn't adhere to a linear curve. It instead follows an asymptotic curve in which purchasing or selling an asset becomes increasingly expensive for the user.

This is shown in Figure 12.3.

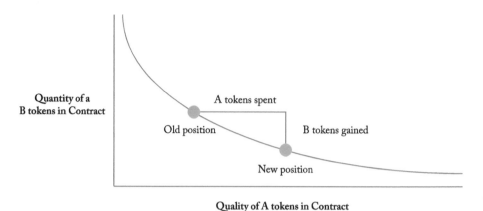

Figure 12.3: Asymptotic curve of tokens in contract

Beyond the AMM structure discussed above, some DEX protocols use the traditional central limit order book model, as used by centralized exchanges. New protocols are emerging to address the AMM capital efficiency problem that introduces an entirely different model for providing liquidity.

Popular decentralized exchanges

Uniswap

Uniswap is a fully decentralized on-chain protocol for a token exchange on Ethereum that uses liquidity pools instead of order books. Anyone can quickly swap between Ethereum and any ERC20 token or earn fees by supplying any amount of liquidity.

You can create a market by providing an equal value of ETH and another ERC-20 token. Uniswap allows only one market per ERC-20 token, and anyone on the Uniswap exchange can be a liquidity provider. Liquidity pool tokens, referred to as LP tokens, are minted once the liquidity is deposited into the system, and tokens are burned after withdrawal. By a constant product formula, the first version of Uniswap has a unique liquidity-sensitive automated pricing mechanism. Uniswap version two (V2) made improvements to the original DEX by allowing trading pairs between any two tokens.

Trading pairs are assets traded for each other, like ETH/DAI.

In Uniswap V2, any ERC-20 token can be pooled directly with any other ERC-20 token. As a result, wrapped Ethereum (WETH) is used in the core contracts instead of native ETH, although end users can still use conventional Ethereum through helper contracts. WETH is a synthetic ERC-20 token tied to the price of Ethereum.

In the summer of 2021, Uniswap launched V3, which is more capital-efficient and introduces concentrated liquidity order books.

This will provide deeper liquidity for trades on the platform by concentrating liquidity to where most trades are occurring.

SushiSwap

SushiSwap is a fork of Uniswap. The community members didn't like the fact that Uniswap was a decentralized project backed by venture capitalists, so the anonymous developers took the open source code of Uniswap and launched their own version of it, introducing a token called SUSHI.

The SUSHI token was never for sale — it had to be earned by using the product. Despite originally being a fork of Uniswap, SushiSwap has added a lot of new products to its platform, and is now one of the most popular DEXs in all of crypto.

Bancor

Bancor is a fully on-chain liquidity protocol. It's different from traditional exchanges because it doesn't charge fees, and furthermore, it has no counterparty. This means that a single party can complete its own transactions. Traditional exchanges typically require two parties to be involved in transactions in real-time.

Bancor also offers no spread, an easy-to-use user interface, and continuous liquidity. The buying and selling prices of Bancor tokens are the same, and the tokens are available anytime, regardless of the trading volume.

Liquidity pools and impermanent loss

In traditional centralized exchanges, entities known as market makers provide liquidity to the bid and ask side of the market in order to facilitate low-slippage trading. Anyone can become a market maker on a DEX by providing any amount of liquidity to a liquidity pool. They earn money for doing so — the revenue streams for a liquidity provider go as follows:

- **Pool trading fees:** The trading fees generated by spot trading in the liquidity pool get distributed based on the relative share of liquidity by liquidity providers.

- **Incentivized pool rewards:** Providing liquidity to a pool that is incentivized with governance token rewards.

But the fundamental problem in providing liquidity on decentralized exchanges is one known as impermanent loss. Impermanent loss is the difference in profit between someone who simply holds the underlying asset and a liquidity provider providing liquidity to a 50:50 pair on a DEX. Suppose an asset

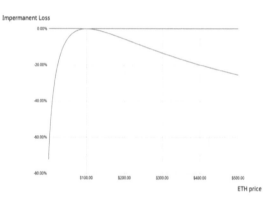

Figure 12.4: Impermanent loss from ETH price change starting from $100/ETH

enters a volatile phase of the market and the price appreciates. In that case, the liquidity providers will suffer impermanent loss (Figure 12.4), meaning they would have been better off holding the asset itself instead of providing liquidity.

This is an important risk to be aware of if you want to be a liquidity provider on a DEX. Automated market makers aim to solve this problem by making everything more capital-efficient, meaning LPs earn trading fees on small amounts of capital.

DEX aggregators

Multiple DEXs have emerged in the DeFi ecosystem, and liquidity often migrates between them based on the various incentives used to attract liquidity providers. This functionality protects against impermanent loss, so an asset's liquidity across DEXs is constantly changing. Users are continually searching for the best pricing and slippage for a trade.

DEX aggregators solve this problem by monitoring liquidity pools across decentralized exchanges and routing an order across DEXs to get the best rate for spot trades. Multiple protocols facilitate this service (like 1inch protocol and Paraswap) and they have been gaining popularity among DeFi users, as shown by the data plotted in Figure 12.5.

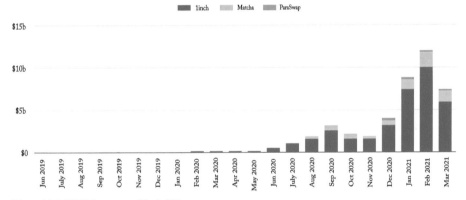

Figure 12.5: DEX Aggregator Trade Volume

Yield aggregators

What is yield farming?

Since the launch of Compound's governance token COMP, DeFi users have had the ability to accumulate a protocol's governance token by providing liquidity or interacting with the protocol's smart contracts to be eligible for an airdrop. This has become known as yield farming in the crypto community — idle assets are used productively to improve a protocol's financial services, and liquidity providers receive that protocol's governance token as a reward.

Many complex yield farming strategies emerged during the bull market of summer 2020. Yield farmers would orchestrate complex asset flows, depositing assets in multiple DeFi protocols to maximize yield and earn multiple governance tokens.

Yearn Finance

Yearn Finance became a crucial player in the yield farming ecosystem with its leading vault products, allocating capital according to the vault's programmatic strategy. DeFi users could now earn high interest on their idle crypto assets. Strategies for achieving this ranged from simply rebalancing stablecoins for the best yields in different money market protocols to earning multiple governance by providing liquidity to Curve Finance's sBTC/wBTC/renBTC vault, for example.

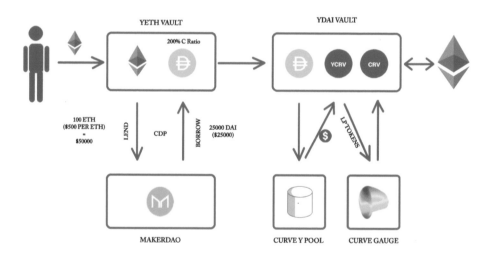

Figure 12.6: YEarn ETH Vault - Current Strategy

For the average user, these yield farming strategies are likely too complex to understand. But fully understanding the strategy is not a prerequisite to earning yield on your assets. The Yearn Finance dApp (Figure 12.6) makes depositing your assets into the vault products as easy as transferring funds. The interest earned by the vault is variable and will most likely change over time.

Derivatives and synthetic assets

What are derivatives?

Cryptocurrency derivatives emerged on centralized exchanges, allowing traders to gain leveraged exposure to an underlying asset. For example, a perpetual contract on BTC/USD lets a trader borrow more BTC from the exchange broker to increase their position size. This is commonly called leveraged trading. DeFi now has decentralized exchanges for spot trading, and is lately on the verge of having DEXs for derivative products.

Derivatives come in many different forms, but futures contracts and perpetual swap contracts are the norm. Futures contracts have a defined date of expiry in which a trader has to close their leveraged position, but a perpetual contract has an indefinite expiry — theoretically, the position can be left open forever.

What are synthetic assets?

Synthetic assets were pioneered by Synthetix. Its native SNX token works as collateral to let users mint "synths," which can be thought of as a temporary on-chain asset representing a real-world asset. This could include shares of Tesla stock, various commodities, fiat indices, and of course crypto assets. Like any other asset, synths can be traded and let users construct a diversified portfolio that includes assets going far beyond cryptocurrency.

How do derivatives work in DeFi?

Exchanges use two models in DeFi. The first is the central limit order book model, used by centralized exchanges.

This model shows the amount of limit buy orders (bids) and limit sell orders (asks) at different prices to construct an order book. The second is the automated market maker model, outlined in a previous section. DeFi protocols can use both of these models to facilitate derivative trading.

For example, dYdX uses an order book model while Perpetual Protocol uses a modified version of the AMM model.

There are two problems to solve for derivative protocols. The first is liquidity — are there enough assets available at any time for large orders to get filled at the specified price?

The other problem is the on-chain speed. Ethereum transactions take time to process and depend on the transaction fee you include. The higher the transaction fee, the faster the transaction gets confirmed.

In its current form, derivative trading on-chain is far more expensive than derivative trading on a centralized exchange. Therefore, derivative protocols need to integrate a layer-2 scalability solution to make transactions significantly cheaper while processing them almost instantaneously.

At Token Metrics, we believe the next significant narrative in the DeFi ecosystem will revolve around derivatives. Knowledge in this domain could reveal the next wave of profitable investments in DeFi.

Decentralized asset management protocols

What is asset management?

In the world of traditional finance, high net worth individuals have access to strong asset managers because they can meet the high capital requirements for participating in a hedge fund or other asset management structure. This means most individuals are unable to access top-tier investment talent, and are instead required to manage their own portfolio or get a less qualified person to do it. In the world of DeFi, investment opportunities are becoming democratized by incentivizing asset managers to manage pools of crypto assets with superior returns.

How does asset management work in DeFi?

Synthetic assets enabled by Synthetix's protocol lets a user gain exposure to real-world assets directly on-chain. But in portfolio management, an asset manager will need access to leveraged derivatives to increase exposure to an asset, or to simply hedge the portfolio of assets using put options to balance the risk.

Decentralized asset management can use core DeFi infrastructure like DEXs, decentralized derivatives, and on-chain synthetic assets to construct a portfolio aimed at producing the highest returns.

A pool manager is incentivized to manage the portfolio transparently, as all transactions can be traced on-chain. Trust is completely removed from the equation, and every asset remains in the custody of the investors, not the asset manager.

DHedge: a decentralized asset management protocol

DHedge is a protocol built on top of Synthetix that uses synthetic assets and a synthetic stablecoin called sUSD to let investors allocate capital to a pool controlled by a pool manager. The pool manager has a right to set a performance fee in which the profit generated will be returned to the pool manager for their efforts.

Investors can allocate any amount of capital they wish, and spread it across multiple pools to diversify their portfolio if the pool manager performs suboptimally. The incentive structure that DHedge uses benefits both the pool managers and the investors themselves. Pool managers are incentivized to make the best returns on the pooled capital from inventors via the performance fee.

Instead of restricting pool access to high net worth individuals, the larger the amount of capital in a pool, the higher the returns are to the pool manager. So open access to the pool without capital requirements helps democratize investment talent and produce higher returns for the managers.

The democratization of finance means lower-income individuals get access to the same opportunities usually reserved for high net worth individuals: higher yields, better asset management, transparency, and verifiability in all financial transactions.

DeFi tutorials

Money market protocols

The tutorial below will cover how to earn interest by depositing crypto assets into an Aave money market. The Aave dApp (Figure 12.7) will display a range of money markets for crypto assets, including the APY on deposits and the APR for borrowing.

You can enter a market by clicking on it — you'll see the market's reserve status and a number of statistics pertaining to the money market, like its reserve size and utilization rate (the ratio between borrowed and available liquidity).

Figure 12.7: Aave dApp interface

In this example, we will be depositing 1,000 USDC into the Aave V2 USDC money market.

- Once you're on the desired money market, click the "deposit" button. This will take you to a page that requires two transactions. The first is the approved transaction, letting the Aave smart contract spend the USDC wallet on your behalf.

- Simply click the "approve" button and send this transaction via your connected wallet.

- After this transaction has been confirmed, you can now deposit USDC into Aave by clicking the "deposit" button.

- Specify how much of the asset you want to deposit, then click the button and once again confirm the transaction within your connected wallet.

- After this transaction has been confirmed, your connected wallet should receive the corresponding amount of interest-bearing Aave tokens.

- Your wallet should now contain 1,000 aUSDC. You can redeem your assets anytime you want using the same process in the Aave application.

Decentralized exchanges

Spot trading via Uniswap

In this DEX example, we will use Uniswap (Figure 12.8) because it is a popular choice for new DeFi users making their first trade.

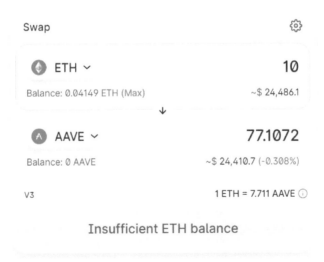

Figure 12.8: Uniswap interface

- As with every dApp, the first step is to connect your wallet by clicking the "connect your wallet" button at the top right of the application.

- After your wallet has been connected, we can proceed with the token swap. The interface shows the asset you will be swapping from (the top box) and the asset you will be swapping to (the bottom box). In our example, we will swap 10 ETH for AAVE (Figure 12.8).

- After inputting the amount of ETH we want to swap, Uniswap will return the estimated amount of AAVE the user wants to receive. We can also see the price impact from our swap, meaning we'll know the slippage that the trade will incur and the fee that will go to the liquidity provider. This can be thought of as the fee required to execute the swap.

- Once the balances are set up correctly, you can swap the tokens by clicking on the swap button and executing the transaction from within your browser wallet or hardware wallet, specifying the amount of gas you want to spend on the transaction.

- If you are swapping one ERC-20 for another, you may need to submit an approved transaction as standard practice for letting Uniswap transfer tokens from your account on the smart contract's behalf.

- After this transaction has been finalized, you are free to execute the swap transaction.

Providing liquidity

DEXs let any user provide liquidity to a trading pair in equal quantities at a 50:50 ratio. This means that for any trades conducted in this liquidity pool, your share of liquidity will be eligible to receive the transaction fees accumulated through other people's swaps.

- To provide liquidity to a trading pair, simply ensure your wallet is connected to the application, then migrate to the Pool page.

- You will be greeted with a page that offers more information about providing liquidity, and a button labeled "Add Liquidity" (Figure 12.9), which will direct you to a page where you can execute the transaction.

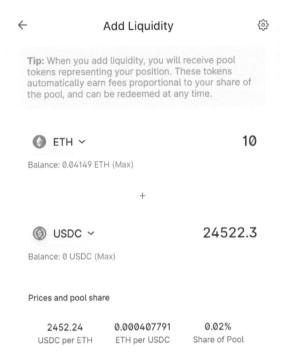

Figure 12.9: Uniswap interface

- Providing liquidity is the exact same process as swapping an asset. Simply choose the two assets you want to provide liquidity for, displaying your share of the liquidity pool.

- If each asset is an ERC-20, it will require an additional approved transaction to let the DEX spend assets on your behalf.

- After the assets have been approved, you can now provide liquidity by clicking the "Supply" button and executing the transaction from within your wallet.

As stated in the section covering decentralized exchanges, the risk of impermanent loss is always there when you provide liquidity to a DEX. You should therefore be aware of such risks when deciding to provide liquidity.

Yield aggregators

Yearn Finance

Yearn Finance offers numerous products to help DeFi users maximize yield on their crypto assets. It's a lending protocol aggregator in which stablecoins are deposited into different lending protocols and rebalanced into the protocols with the highest yield.

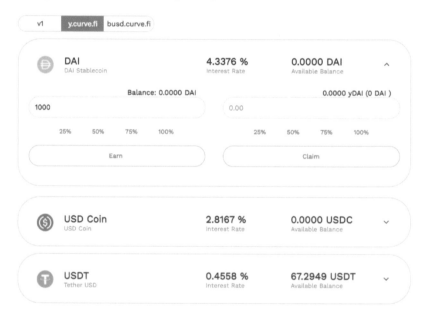

Figure 12.10: Yearn Finance interface

- To begin earning yield on your stablecoins, first navigate to the Yearn Finance dApp and click "Invest - Earn."

- First choose the stablecoin you want to earn yield on, then make sure you have that stablecoin in your wallet. This only requires a simple DEX swap transaction.

- Enter the amount of the stablecoins you want to deposit and click "Earn" to confirm the transaction. Yearn will move stablecoins from your wallet to the smart contract, earning you the corresponding amount of yDAI or which stablecoin you chose.

- Once that's complete, your stablecoins are now earning yield across the DeFi ecosystem, entirely automated by Yearn Finance.

YVault

Instead of rebalancing assets between lending protocols to find the best yield on stablecoins, YVault lets you earn yield on assets beyond stablecoins. Simply navigate to the Yearn Finance dApp, enter the "Invest - Vaults" page, and choose which vault you want to join.

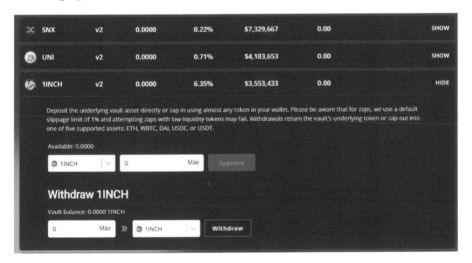

Figure 12.11: YEarn Finance Vault Interface

In this example, we will be using our idle 1Inch tokens to invest in the 1Inch vault.

- First, make sure you hold 1Inch tokens in your connected wallet.

- Specify the amount of tokens you want to deposit into the vault, then click approve.

- Once the approved transaction has been confirmed, click "deposit" to deposit your tokens into the vault.

- Upon depositing the asset, you will receive a vault token that can be redeemed for your assets plus the interest at any time.

Decentralized asset management

Enter a DHedge pool

Figure 12.12: DHedge pool interface

- Navigate to the DHedge application and connect your browser or hardware wallet to the application using the "Connect Wallet" button in the top right of the application.

- Explore some of the DHedge pools using the Leaderboard in the Explore section, as shown in Figure 12.12

- We can sort these pools based on performance, the total value they contain, their risk factor, and performance fees.

- After determining which pool you want to invest in, make sure you have the sUSD stablecoin. It is easily acquired through a DEX swap.

- Click on the pool, then click on the invest button to execute the pool investment transaction, entering the amount of sUSD you want to invest into the pool.

- After the transaction is finalized, you will receive liquidity provider tokens that represent your relative share of liquidity in the pool.

- These tokens can be redeemed for the sUSD you invested at any time.

Pros

Transparency

Users develop smart contracts to store their lending and borrowing transactions on the blockchain, making transactions transparent.

Accessibility

Some countries lack a mature banking system, and some people's circumstances might have them locked out of conventional banking altogether. But anyone anywhere can access a DeFi platform. The barriers to lending and borrowing are far lower in DeFi than they are with traditional financial institutions.

Minimization of credit risk

When users borrow tokens on DeFi platforms, they need to use their crypto as collateral. This reduces the credit risk of each transaction, even if there's no third party to supervise it.

Cons

Ethereum dependency

A common problem among DeFi platforms is that most of them are built on Ethereum, so they are highly dependent on the Ethereum blockchain. DeFi platforms might not guarantee decentralization once they create their own mainnet.

Smart contract vulnerabilities

The code for smart contracts is public, so they are open books for someone looking to maliciously take advantage of any potential exploits. But this problem is common for any blockchain, not just for DeFi platforms.

The bottom line

Decentralized finance is an emerging category of fintech focused on interoperability, accessibility, and fast liquidation. The DeFi market is still in an early stage, but we can see how it stands to transform traditional banking systems — its advantages are more significant than its drawbacks.

CHAPTER 13

Introduction to Mining and Staking

Introduction to Mining and Staking

Blockchains often operate like distributed computing systems. Network nodes need to communicate with each other to stay on the same page. The transparent communication method between nodes is known as consensus. The consensus method is a protocol for maintaining the ledger's consistent state, and it lies at the heart of a blockchain. The consensus in a blockchain is to order the transactions in the ledger and prevent double-spending. Consensus mechanisms link participants and procedures associated with consenting transactions on a chain. They function to guarantee a blockchain transaction's authenticity and validity.

According to Edward Shils' "The Concept Of Consensus," there are three things necessary for consensus:

1. A standard agreement of laws, rules, and norms.

2. A sense of unity and identity to aid group members in understanding they are equal.

3. A standard agreement of institutions that apply these laws and rules.

Consensus algorithms let linked machines work together to survive if one of its members fails. This tolerance of failure is another significant advantage of blockchains and distributed ledgers.

How consensus mechanisms work

Basic parameters that define consensus mechanism are:

- Decentralized governance – A single central authority cannot grant transaction finality.

- Quorum structure – Nodes can exchange messages in distinct ways.

- Integrity – It implements the authentication of transaction integrity.

- Authentication – This procedure offers a method of verifying the participants' identities.

- Nonrepudiation – This procedure verifies that the supposed sender actually sent the message.

- Privacy – It helps guarantee that only the expected recipient can read the sent messages.

- Fault tolerance – It helps guarantee that the network operates efficiently and rapidly.

- Performance – It considers throughput, liveness, scalability, and latency.

Implementation of the parameters mentioned above happens by way of private keys, hashing functions, and hierarchical deterministic keys.

Different blockchain consensus mechanisms

Proof of Work

As the first blockchain consensus mechanism, Proof of Work (PoW) is what drives Bitcoin. Several cryptocurrencies have followed BTC's footsteps and adopted this same consensus mechanism.

As found in the Bitcoin blockchain, PoW depends on network participants to reach a consensus by calculating hash functions, tricky mathematical puzzles that require lots of computational power. The first miner to decipher the puzzle gets to create a block and receives a reward for doing so.

These mathematical puzzles have some interesting properties:

- They are asymmetric, meaning it takes a lot of time to find the solution.

- The only way to decipher these puzzles is to "guess" the answer. Therefore, if a miner wants to enter lots of guesses for an increased chance of winning, they need more computational power.

- The block mining speed depends on the difficulty of these puzzles. Blocks have to be created within a specific time frame to maintain a steady supply of new coins. The puzzles get more challenging if they're produced too quickly, and they get less demanding if produced slowly.

With bitcoin as a reward, miners achieve consensus by working to validate multiple transactions in a block.

A significant problem with using PoW for blockchain consensus protocols is the substantial amount of computing power and electricity needed for mining. The systems that mine Bitcoin successfully can be enormously expensive to operate.

Proof of Stake

The undesirable cost of mining led to the development of other consensus mechanisms. Proof of Stake (PoS) is considerably cheaper than PoW, as it doesn't need supercharged processing power to be successful. Instead, cryptocurrency holders with the most assets are in charge of achieving consensus.

PoS can be likened to voting power among shareholders of a company. The number of shares owned by a person determines their voting power and influence. PoS applies the same idea, but with crypto assets instead of shares of stock. Those with the most coins in a PoS chain determine which new data is added to the blockchain. Ideally, the person holding the most coins would most likely want to ensure the chain's safety. They are called validators, as opposed to miners.

But just like miners, validators are rewarded for their work with that chain's currency.

Delegated Proof of Stake

Delegated Proof of Stake (DPoS) is a consensus algorithm that's often considered a more efficient and democratic version of the proof of stake mechanism.

DPoS is a blockchain consensus model formed around democracy. Members of a blockchain choose who approves transactions. The delegates' identities are often known — these people are usually selected based upon their merits in the chain and how many coins they hold.

DPoS differs significantly from PoS. By validating transactions within a single source in a chain, it reduces the power needed to solve the transactions' blockchain consensus algorithms.

Like miners, those delegated through DPoS also receive payment for their work based on the platform they are using. Payment rates and the number of delegates that can be selected differ depending on the platform.

For instance, in the BitShares blockchain, the minimum number of delegates is 11.

Here is how DPoS works:

- Block production happens in sets of 21.

- 21 block producers are chosen from the pool of block producer candidates. An automatic selection of the top twenty occurs, while the 21st is selected proportional to their votes.

- The producers shuffle around using a somewhat random number derived from the block time. This is to keep balanced connectivity to all other producers.

- Producers who don't participate aren't considered. This is to ensure that block production stays regular — a producer must produce a minimum of one block every 24 hours.

Hybrid PoW/PoS

The hybrid blockchain attempts to use the best of both private and public blockchain solutions. In an ideal world, a hybrid blockchain allows for controlled access and freedom at the same time.

Hybrid blockchains aren't open to everyone, but still offers classic blockchain features like integrity, transparency, and security. They are entirely customizable as well. Members of a hybrid blockchain decide who can participate or which transactions are public, merging the best of the private and public worlds.

What is Staking

Staking is the process of actively participating in transaction validation (similar to mining) on a Proof of Stake blockchain. On these blockchains, anyone with a minimum required balance of a specific cryptocurrency can validate transactions and earn staking rewards.

When the minimum balance is met, a node deposits that amount of cryptocurrency into the network as a stake, similar to a security deposit. The size of a stake is directly proportional to the chances of that node being chosen to forge the next block. If the node successfully creates a block, then the validator receives a reward, similar to how a miner is rewarded under Proof of Work. Validators lose part of their stake if they double-sign or attempt to attack the network.

Market liquidity

Studies show that a higher staking yield can create negative pressure on market liquidity. In simpler terms, pushing monetary investments within cryptocurrency eliminates dependence on fiat currency like cash.

Market prices

High staking yields can introduce a bullish market bias. Investor confidence will be at an all-time high, as they feel optimistic about the increasing value of the coins that they hold.

It is important to remember that this bias is inherent in investor behavior, not the market as a whole. Buyers who act upon this bias can eventually lose a lot more money than they initially expected. Investors should therefore do their research and due diligence, as cryptocurrency prices are volatile.

What to stake

The growing popularity of staking has given rise to tons of options for users interested in earning passive income with idle crypto assets. Some of the prominent cryptocurrencies offering staking rewards right now are:

Ethereum 2.0

Ethereum (ETH), the second most popular cryptocurrency, has announced its long-awaited staking options under Ethereum 2.0. Early validators can essentially help the system flourish by staking a minimum of 32 ETH. You can start by heading over to the Eth2 LaunchPad to get more details.

Tezos (XTZ)

In June 2018, Tezos (XTZ) won major attention with a prominent ICO that generated over $230 million in investment. It implemented a version of PoS referred to as liquid proof-of-stake (LPoS). XTZ calls its staking process "baking." Bakers get compensated with the native Tezos coin. Bakers who misbehave on the network are penalized by having their stake taken from them.

A user needs to have 8,000 XTZ coins and run a full node in order to become a staker/baker on Tezos. Luckily, third-party services let small coin holders delegate smaller portions of XTZ and share baking rewards. The annual percentage yield on XTZ staking varies between 5-6%.

Algorand (ALGO)

Algorand's (ALGO) goal is to drive reduced-cost cross-border payments. As a PoS protocol, the network needs stakers for transaction and security processing. Although it implements the pure proof-of-stake (PPoS) consensus mechanism, it still requires stakers to run full nodes.

There are third parties who support ALGO delegation. The annual staking rewards on these networks vary between 5-10%. For instance, people staking on Binance earn an APY of eight percent.

Icon (ICX)

Icon (ICX) is a complex Korean blockchain project that uses the DPoS consensus algorithm, unlike Algorand and Tezos. Only a select number of users find new blocks and validate transactions, while others allocate their coins to these entities. Annual staking rewards on ICX vary between 6-36%.

Where to stake

Exchanges

Thanks to the sizable number of users on their platforms, exchanges have naturally jumped into the staking business. Staking lets investors expand their income stream and monetize unused funds on exchanges. Prominent cryptocurrency exchanges that support staking include:

- **Binance** – Binance is the most prominent digital currency exchange by trading volume and many investors use this platform for staking. It introduced staking for Ethereum 2.0 in December 2020, and supports staking for other cryptos like Binance USD (BUSD), Binance Coin (BNB), Tether (USDT), BTC, and DAI.

- **Coinbase** – Coinbase, another leading cryptocurrency exchange, offers staking options for a number of cryptocurrencies including ETH 2.0, ALGO, and XTZ.

Cold/private wallet

Let's talk about "cold staking." The user must leave staked coins at the same address — moving them breaks the lock-up period, which subsequently causes them to lose staking rewards. Prominent offline/private cryptocurrency wallets accommodating staking include:

- **Ledger** – Ledger is the industry leader for cold wallets. Its hardware wallets let the user retain complete control of their coins during a staking session. Ledger users can stake up to seven coins. It supports staking for Tron (TRX), ATOM, and ALGO, among others.

- **Trust Wallet** – The multipurpose Trust Wallet is a private wallet supported by Binance. The wallet lets users earn passive income by staking IoTeX (IOTX), ALGO, XTZ, VeChain (VET), TRX, Callisto (CLO), TomoChain (TOMO), and ATOM.

- **CoolWallet S** – CoolWallet S offers its users stablecoin staking for USDT through its X-Savings feature.

- **Trezor** – The world's first hardware wallet supports the staking of assets like Tezos via thirty-party apps like the Exodus wallet.

Staking-as-a-Service Platforms

Staking-as-a-service platforms are not like cryptocurrency exchanges or wallets. They exist entirely to enable staking, and they take a percentage of earned rewards as a fee. Staking on these platforms is referred to as soft staking.

- Stake Capital – Staking for Cosmos (ATOM), Aion (AION), Livepeer (LPT), KAVA, XTZ, and Loom Network (LOOM) are supported on this platform.

- MyCointainer – Users on the "MyCointainer" platform can choose between the Power Max, Power Plus, and Basic options when staking their assets. Basic users are charged as little as $1, while those on the Power Max plan pay more than $10 per month. The platform supports staking for over fifty cryptocurrencies and on-chain staking support.

DeFi Staking

- Maker (MKR) – Users are allowed to loan stablecoins against a volatile cryptocurrency like bitcoin. According to DeFi Pulse, this prominent decentralized finance protocol is ranked number one in total volume locked (TVL) as of March 2021. The network uses DAI as its primary stablecoin. Yield farmers deposit DAI, which is loaned out to borrowers, and they receive rewards from the interest fees on those loans.

- Synthetix (SNX) – Synthetix has a native currency named SNX. The platform issues synthetic assets, known as synths. Synths are virtual assets used to characterize physical and real-world assets like stocks, cryptos, and fiat currencies.

- Yearn Finance (YFI) – This DeFi aggregator came into existence in February 2020. The aim is to lower risk by distributing deposited funds into platforms with the best yields. It allocates funds between Aave and Compound to provide the highest yield.

- Compound (COMP) – Compound lets users borrow or lend a small range of cryptocurrencies like Basic Attention Token (BAT), USD Coin (USDC), DAI, and ETH. It uses lending pools and charges interest on loans. For collateral, the protocol compels borrowers to deposit a stipulated amount of supported coins.

How to choose a staking platform

1. When using new DeFi platforms, do your research on Reddit and Twitter to see what others think about the protocol. Don't just jump in based on what the team or founders say. Technically savvy investors might spot a potential rug pull and alert community members to any signs of foul play.

2. Beyond annualized rewards or APYs, focus on factors like the platform's reputation and age.

3. Use trustworthy platforms like Maker or Cool Wallet instead of risking your crypto assets on untested platforms that promise incredibly high staking yields.

4. Use dependable analytics like CoinMarketCap to analyze information on PoS-based platforms, staking-as-a-service platforms, and third-party staking services.

5. Read all the rules, terms, and conditions about the staking process before jumping in. Find out if you need your wallet connected to the internet all the time, if there is a cooling period before unstaking, a minimum amount to stake, and so on.

How to stake crypto

Staking on an exchange

Using Binance as our staking platform and Ethereum as our cryptocurrency, let's look at how to stake crypto using an exchange.

- First you must have a Binance account and the cryptocurrency Ether (ETH). If you don't have any, you can buy them on an exchange or swap them for other coins.

- When logged in, go to Finance > Binance Earn > ETH 2.0 staking.

- Staked ETH coins have a lock-up duration of up to twenty-four months. Binance tokenizes the staked ETH and dispenses rewards as BETH.

- Click "Stake Now" and enter the amount of ETH you want to stake.

- Hit "Confirm," read the terms and conditions that appear, then hit "Confirm" again.

Staking on a hardware wallet

Staking crypto on a hardware wallet like Ledger is relatively straight-forward.

- Download and install the app pertaining to the coin you want to stake.

- Open Ledger Live, create a new account, and migrate the coins you want to stake using Ledger Live.

Risk and rewards of staking

Staking reward rates are calculated based on the duration or maturity period selected. Although different coins have different rates, the mechanism is often the same: the longer you hold your coins, the higher your reward.

For instance:

- **3 months: +10%**
- **6 months: +25%**
- **12 months: +70%**

Annual rewards could change, so do your research before staking your crypto.

The bottom line

PoW, PoS, and DPoS are the most prominent and developed forms of consensus out there. Staking requires few resources, unlike conventional crypto mining. You don't need to burn lots of electricity or buy a super-charged computer to participate.

CHAPTER 14

Introduction to
Non-Fungible Tokens (NFTs)

CHAPTER 14

Introduction to
Non-Fungible Tokens (NFTs)

NFTs exploded in popularity during the COVID-19 pandemic, as enthusiasts and investors scurried to buy digital items that only exist online.

If you've ever purchased tickets to a concert or bought baseball cards, then you are already familiar with non-fungible commodities. These goods aren't interchangeable because certain unique qualities about them add to or reduce their value. For example, a baseball card's condition affects its value, and the location of a seat at a concert affects ticket price.

A study released by a non-fungible token market analyst firm Non-Fungible.com stated the total value of all NFT transactions (including minting, breeding, and renting) skyrocketed from $62 million in 2019 to $250 million in 2020. NFT traders have also mostly seen extraordinary gains in the same timeframe, with profits of up to $500,000 in a single year and individual traders making six-figure income trading NFTs.

In October 2020, Miami-based art collector Pablo Rodriguez-Fraile paid nearly $67,000 for a 10-second video artwork that he could have streamed for free online. He sold it in February 2021 for $6.6 million, almost a 1,000% profit.

The thriving NFT market has seen big brands entering to create lucrative NFT-based goods and services. These include brands like the NBA, Formula 1, Louis Vuitton, Nike, IBM, the BBC, and many more. Interest in this sector is undeniable.

What are non-fungible tokens?

NFTs are a sort of cryptographic token on a blockchain that embody a unique asset.

Chapter 14 Introduction to Non-Fungible Tokens (NFTs)
// 197 //

They can either be completely digital assets, or tokenized versions of assets that exist in the real world. As NFTs are not interchangeable, they can prove authenticity and ownership within the digital realm.

Fungibility means that an asset's units are interchangeable and practically indistinguishable from one other. Fiat currencies are fungible, for example, because each unit is interchangeable with any other equivalent individual unit. A $20 bill is worth the same as any other $20 bill.

This is an essential feature for any asset filling a role as a means of exchange. Fungibility grants free exchange, and there is theoretically no way to know the history of each individual unit. But that makes it an undesirable characteristic for high-dollar collectible items.

Imagine if we could create a digital asset that's similar to Bitcoin, but each unit had a unique identifier associated with it. This would make each of them different from all the other units — in other words, they become non-fungible.

Non-fungible token standards

ERC-721

In 2017, Dieter Shirley outlined ERC-721 tokens in an Ethereum Improvement Proposal (EIP). First used by CryptoKitties, ERC-721 was the first standard to represent non-fungible digital assets.

ERC-721 is a transferable solidity smart contract standard, so developers can simply create new ERC721-compliant contracts by importing them from the OpenZeppelin library. This standard maps unique identifiers to addresses representing the owner of that identifier. It also permits the transfer of these assets using the "transferFrom" method.

These two methods are all you need to characterize an NFT: a way to check who owns it, and a way to transfer it to a new owner.

ERC-1155

ERC-1155, pioneered by the Enjin team, brings the idea of semi-fungibility to the NFT world. Under this standard, IDs denote classes of assets as opposed to single assets.

For instance, an ID might represent "blades," and a wallet could own 6,000 of these blades. In this case, the "balanceOf" method would return the number of blades owned by a wallet, and the user can transfer any number of these blades by calling "transferFrom" with the "blade" ID.

It's an efficient system. If a user wanted to transfer 6,000 blades under the ERC-721 standard, they would need to change the smart contract's state (by calling the "transferFrom" method) for 6,000 unique tokens. But under ERC-1155, the developer only needs to call "transferFrom" with a quantity of 6,000 and execute a single transaction.

This increased capability comes with a loss of information. The user can't trace the history of an individual blade.

Composables

Composables, led by the ERC-998 standard, provide a template by which NFTs can own fungible and non-fungible assets. There have only been a few composable NFTs deployed on the mainnet.

Non-Ethereum standards

Although it seems like most NFTs are born on Ethereum, there are several other NFT standards pertaining to other chains.

DGoods, introduced by the Mythical Games team, is a feature-rich cross-chain standard that started with EOS.

The Cosmos project is also creating an NFT module that can be used as part of the Cosmos SDK.

Characteristics of NFTs

- Digital ownership – People who have NFTs in their wallets own and control the NFT.

- Permanent – NFTs have data permanently stored within the token. This information includes images, messages, signatures, or any other data.

- Permissionless – NFTs can be built on a permissionless blockchain like Ethereum.

- Programmable – An NFT is just a selection of code on a blockchain. It can be programmed to have several attributes. For example, an NFT artwork might be programmed to pay the artist royalties on every secondary sale of that artwork.

- Unique – NFTs are unique, and that uniqueness can be confirmed on a blockchain.

Examples of NFT projects and sectors

The first non-fungible tokens were created in 2016 for crypto-collectible trading card games before ERC-721 was accepted as a digital token standard.

Art and marketplaces

Art is a rapidly growing NFT niche. Painters, designers, musicians, and more create NFTs via blockchain-based minting platforms to retain more control over their creative output.

SuperRare

SuperRare (SR) is one of Ethereum's debut crypto-art NFT marketplaces. Artists must be accepted to the platform before they can participate. The team currently handpicks a roster of artists, as SR is still in early access

Crypto Investing Guide

mode. You can discover tokenized digital art, buy and sell it, and show-case your collection on the platform.

Nifty Gateway

Nifty Gateway is owned by the Gemini crypto exchange and has be-come one of NFT ecosystem's most prevalent marketplaces. They focus on user-friendly and viral drops by celebrated artists like Beeple, Trevor Jones, Pak, and more. In February 2021, Nifty Gateway clocked over $55 million in sales volume.

Rarible

Rarible is a do-it-yourself NFT marketplace where you can mint NFTs when and how you please. Creators are highly favorable toward Rarible, as the minting process is free, easy, and unrestricted. Rarible's native governance token "RARI" is used to incentivize platform users and give the community members a voice. That unrestricted access means Rarible has become a place for people to mint counterfeit versions of existing NFTs and pass them off as the original. To an extent, this is an inevita-ble reality of DIY minting platforms.

Async Art

Async Art is a unique art platform on Ethereum centered around program-mable art that launched in February 2020. Async pieces have Master and Layer tokens. On Async, digital paintings can be split into "layers," stacked on each other to establish new appearances in the Master image.

Art Blocks

Art Blocks is an on-demand generative art platform built on Ethereum. Artists and creators can deploy custom-tailored algorithms to the mar-ketplace for limited-edition drops. If users make a purchase while a drop is live, an algorithm executes and creates a new NFT artwork from the artist's exclusively generated code. The platform charges a 10% fee for the projects listed.

MakersPlace

Initially founded in 2016, MakersPlace is one of the first digital art marketplaces. MakersPlace ties with Known Origin and Foundation for the highest direct commission of 15%.

KnownOrigin

KnownOrigin launched in April 2018. Although it was one of the earlier entrants, it failed to achieve a substantial market share compared to its closest rivals. It is ranked in the lower tier of cryptoart marketplaces by volume.

Foundation

Foundation launched in May 2020 as a marketplace for limited-edition goods where pieces were distributed on a bonding curve. Its NFT sales volume surpasses both KnownOrigin and Async Art.

Collectibles

CryptoPunks

CryptoPunks launched in the summer of 2017 and was the first NFT project released through Ethereum. It cemented the use of the ERC-721 token standard that has since dominated the NFT ecosystem today.

There are only 10,000 unique characters, and they're rare exquisite collectibles. They were initially distributed and claimed for free, but are currently sold on the marketplace with an average sale price of over $72,000 per piece.

CryptoKitties

CryptoKitties launched in 2017, not long after the CryptoPunks. It's a game centered around breeding and trading adorable kittens. You can breed or adopt kittens of all shapes and colors, and they can't be replicated or destroyed.

Aavegotchi

Aavegotchi is a digital collectibles project built by Aave. You can collect Tamagotchi-like monsters, build them up, battle them against each other, or hold them to gain yield — they store interest-bearing DeFi tokens.

Avastars

Avastars is a fully on-chain NFT project created by development studio nft42. Avastars have their media and metadata solely stored on the Ethereum blockchain.

Hashmasks

Hashmasks is the latest digital collectibles project on the NFT scene, but it's already made significant waves. There are a total of 16,384 unique Hashmasks, and each one is a combination of work by varying artists. They have different eye colors, masks, and other attributes that makes them rare.

NBA Top Shot

NBA Top Shot is a blockchain-based trading card system that lets people buy basketball video highlights as NFTs. It has sold over $500 million in NFTs since launch. In February, a LeBron James dunk set the record for the most expensive Top Shot sale at $208,000. You can purchase NFT "packs" for as little as $14.00, and they are often sold out.

Games

Blockchain games are moving towards a future of "play-to-earn." Users can play, earn, and can trade assets within a game.

Axie Infinity

Axie Infinity is an Ethereum game where users can collect, trade, sell, breed, and battle iconic Axie monsters. It's the largest Ethereum game at the moment and one of Ethereum's most-used apps.

Sorare

Sorare is a fast-rising fantasy football game that's made significant progress by partnering with some of the biggest professional football franchises in the world. Players build fantasy squads with digital trading cards and compete to determine the best football team manager around.

Gods Unchained

Players create decks of different fantastical varieties and then battle them to gain on-chain renown and tokenized prizes. According to Rare, Epic, Legendary, and Shiny Legendary, packs are graded and sold as low as $2.49.

Metaverse

Ethereum has let virtual reality (VR) projects make their underlying digital real estate limited and tradable around the world via NFTs.

Decentraland

Decentraland, one of Ethereum's oldest and most used VR projects, lets users trade virtual land. Users can own and trade in a virtual world. The native token MANA is burnt or spent in exchange for these parcels of virtual land.

Cryptovoxels

Cryptovoxels is another of Ethereum's premier VR projects. Users can purchase land, build digital stores, and set up art galleries. Parcels are purchased through OpenSea.

Utility

NFTs can even point to domain names, tweets, and more.

Ethereum Name Service

The Ethereum Name Service (ENS) lets Ethereum users build and operate decentralized domain names on Ethereum. They mint these decentralized domains as NFTs to make them easier to trade. These NFTs make it significantly simpler to manage transactions as opposed to dealing with lengthy alphanumeric wallet addresses.

DeFi and NFTs

The Ethereum ecosystem has seen massive growth and innovation, both in NFTs and DeFi. Some NFT and DeFi protocols are the most talked-about projects.

NFTfi

NFTfi is a marketplace for NFT collateralized loans. Users can lend out their NFTs or use them as collateral. If the borrower defaults, the lender obtains ownership of the underlying NFTs.

NIFTEX

NIFTEX is a protocol used to fractionalize NFTs into simple tradable ERC-20 tokens called shards. Shards are traded on the market like standard cryptocurrencies. To recover the underlying assets, a user would need to acquire 100% of its shards.

Yearn Insurance NFTs

Yearn Insurance NFTs offer smart contract insurance for several protocols. These tokenized insurance policies are traded on NFT marketplaces like OpenSea and Rarible.

How are NFTs created?

Anyone can make an NFT in a few steps.

- Get your media ready. NFTs support a range of files like MP3 audio, JPG, PNG, and GIF images, and even 3D files like GLB.

- Set up an Ethereum Wallet to securely store the cryptocurrency you will use to buy, sell, and create NFTs. Wallets are also important for signing in and creating accounts on NFT marketplaces.

- Buy Ethereum to cover the cost of NFT to be created.

- Connect the wallet to an NFT marketplace like Rarible. Tap the "Connect" button in the top right corner of the screen. Your account is created and you are ready to create, mint, and sell your first NFT.

- Upload your file to the platform and describe your asset. Decide if you would like to create a standalone piece or multiple NFTs of the same piece, royalty, and others. Start minting — the process requires ETH for transaction approvals. Your digital artwork is now ready to be traded and purchased on the marketplace.

What to do with NFTs

NFTs trade on the blockchain, so there's lots of freedom to what can be done with them, including:

- Buying and selling them on a marketplace.

- Trading or gifting them.

- Using them in dApps like games.

- Showcasing your public NFT inventory within a dApp or on social media.

Where to buy NFTs and how to use them

NFTs are available for purchase at several different exchanges, including Rarible, Opensea, and the Worldwide Asset Exchange (WAX). NFTs can also be purchased from the creator directly. For example, Decentraland's LAND tokens are purchased in-game. (For the majority of 2018, LAND tokens had a higher volume than any other non-fungible token.) There is no wrong or right way to use your NFTs, just like there is no right or wrong way to buy, trade, or sell ordinary collectibles. Many owners of the LAND token would tell you that owning LAND is no different than an investor buying proper real-world land.

Gamers might buy NFTs since there are rising use cases for them within gaming. For example, Decentraland lets you put pictures of your CryptoKitties collection on your plot of land. Other uses include buying a weapon in one game and transferring it to be used in another game. Weapons and skins can also be purchased on exchanges such as bitskins.

We are still in the early days of NFTs, but their potential for future growth is limitless and could be potentially massive for the overall crypto market.

Why invest in NFTs?

NFTs have proven to be a beneficial form of investment for the following reasons:

- They provide value for the tokenized asset – NFTs provide a means for physical objects (like artwork) to become tokenized, guarding against forgeries, establishing ownership, and generally protecting the artist's interests. This creates scarcity and increases value.

- They give investors more liquidity.

- They enhance the capacity for growth and development – NFTs offer growth and development for a number of sectors, like real estate. People can own their assets, rent them out, and otherwise decide what they want to do with them.

The future of NFTs

Representing assets and proving their ownership is a crucial functionality for blockchain technology. Digital art, collectibles, and in-game assets are just the start. Our homes have different addresses, our cars have unique VINs, and even people have an individual social security number. NFTs present a new and effective way for people to potentially purchase land, gold, or other non-fungible real-world assets.

The global market cap for gold and real estate exceeds $300 trillion. If even 0.1% of that figure were tokenized, it would nearly double the total crypto market cap.

Tokenized real estate is a massive opportunity for increasing ordinary people's financial independence. Real estate in general is one of the earliest and most lucrative forms of investing, but the entry barriers have become far too great for the average person to meaningfully participate.

Investors in tokenized real estate will be able to put in as much they can afford and still partake in real estate investing.

In 2018, a $30 million Manhattan luxury property became the city's first property on the blockchain. Tokenization of property also lets real estate developers skip the hassle of traditional bank financing, and instead finance their projects through other means.

Nike recently became interested in the NFT field. We don't know exactly what they plan to do, but they recently filed a patent for NFT-enabled sneakers called "CryptoKicks."

In 2019, high-end fashion brand Louis Vuitton announced plans to use NFTs to track the ownership of different luxury fashion items.

They could use NFTs to track the entire history of a bag, from the factory where it was made to the closet where the owner stores it.

NFTs also give us the ability to tokenize things like certifications, degrees, and licenses. This will let us issue, maintain, and track these certifications within a blockchain. Sensitive data like medical records could be tokenized and protected using blockchain technology, giving us greater control over our data.

The real potential for NFTs lies in the ability to immutably show ownership of any non-fungible commodity, whether that commodity is real or virtual.

The bottom line

There is immense interest in NFTs lately. They are permissionless, programmable, and unique. They can transfer data and value on blockchains and facilitate a number of opportunities.

AFTERWORD

—

Congratulations on finishing this book and taking in new knowledge about how to make money in the 21st century! As we finish here, I'd like to think that your own journey to financial freedom is just beginning. Now that you've got a head full of relevant information to make yourself into a deadly crypto trader, the only remaining step is to go out and apply your knowledge.

You might reread a few chapters or do some more of your own research, but knowledge without application is useless: the ball is now in your court to figure out where you fit in this brave new world of crypto investing.

And you're not out there wandering through the wilderness alone — you have all the resources and connections you need to succeed. Come back to this book as necessary, tune into the free Token Metrics livestreams for timely investment info, and subscribe to Token Metrics to gain a meaningful edge in your crypto trading and investing.

We have given you the knowledge and blueprint for profitably investing in crypto and mitigating risk, but none of that matters if you don't apply it. When you do, I believe you will build meaningful wealth for you and your family.

The stage is now set for you to accomplish anything you want in crypto.

The moon is not the limit,
to the moon and beyond!

TOKEN
METRICS

CPSIA information can be obtained
at www.ICGtesting.com
Printed in the USA
BVHW061540011021
617788BV00001BA/1